# How Quantum Physicists Build New Beliefs

### Your Personal Coaching Guide to Truly and Fully Unleash the Law of Attraction

By

# Greg Kuhn

# Table of Contents

**Introduction** ........................................................................ 1

**Chapter One**: What to Expect from This Book and How It Will Help You.............................................................................. 5

**Chapter Two**: An Overview of Your Brain's Actual Functionality and Use.................................................................................. 9

**Chapter Three**: How Your Beliefs Create Your Material Reality.................................................. 15

**Chapter Four**: How You Acquired Your Beliefs and Why Your Subconscious Brain is Like a Scared Bunny ......................... 21

**Chapter Five**: My Process to Retrain Your Subconscious Brain and Build New Beliefs that Align With and Manifest Your Desires......... 27

> **Step One**: Identify How You Currently Feel About Your Chosen Absent Desire.................................................................... 30

> **Step Two**: Select the Next Highest Emotion Up the Chart and Write About Your Absent Desire from that Perspective................................ 33

> **Step Three**: Live Your Way into that Next Highest Emotion Over the Course of One to Three Days (or Longer if You Feel it Necessary) ............................................................................ 35

> **Step Four**: Select the Next Highest Emotion Up the Chart From the One You Just Wrote About/Lived Your Way Into and Write About It/Live Your Way Into It in the Same Manner You Did with the Previous One .......................................................................... 39

> **Step Five**: Never Moving More than One Emotion Up at a Time and Never Moving More than One Emotion Up Per Day, Repeat Steps 2 through 4 Until You Have Moved Yourself All the Way Up to the Top of the Emotional Reference Chart ........................................ 40

**Chapter Six**: Additional Coaching From Questions Asked Most Frequently While Using My Process........................................ 53

**Chapter Seven**: The Story of My Personal Experience with Using My Process for the First Time ................................................ 65

**Chapter Eight**: A Coaching Client's Experience with Using My Process for the First Time.......................................................... 91

**Chapter Nine**: About the Author................................................ 123

# Introduction

When I graduated from college, I moved into a large old home in Keedysville, Maryland, that was so close to Antietam National Battlefield that I could throw a rock across the road and hit it. I agreed to renovate the house in exchange for paying rent so I could save money for graduate school while I worked in nearby Frederick.

One early June Sunday afternoon, taking a lunch break from fixing some holes in the roof, I sat down on my back porch (such as it was). Relaxing and eating a sandwich, I enjoyed my view of some woods that backed up pretty close to the house. Halfway through my roast beef, I noticed a cute little bunny peering from the shrubs about 12 feet away. The little guy seemed to be looking right at me, although in retrospect perhaps his wriggling nose indicated he was more interested in my lunch than me.

I had a compelling thought that I'd like to pet the cute guy. My mother raised Angora rabbits while I was growing up, so I considered myself at least competent with bunnies—wild or not. Grabbing a juicy carrot from my paper plate, I waved it as invitingly as I could and called out in a soft voice, "Here Mr. Bunny. Come and get it."

The little guy was not impressed. And he didn't move a bit. Not that I was surprised. After all, a small wild animal is concerned with one thing and one thing only: safety. And nothing provides safety more reliably than familiar surroundings. I thought to myself, "This bunny doesn't know my intentions and he has no reason to trust me. It wouldn't matter if I was offering him a gourmet carrot soufflé; if he doesn't feel safe, he's not coming over here."

But, since I had the whole summer at my disposal and I'd be living at the house, I decided to try an experiment with the little guy. Could I coax this cute little bunny up onto my back porch? I knew that this rabbit would be very cautious and its survival instincts would tell it to give in very slowly, but I also knew I could probably tempt him if I kept offering him some delicious fare.

The key would be to feed him on a regular basis and incrementally inch the food a little closer to the porch each time. If I moved the food almost imperceptibly closer each day, before the summer ended the bunny might actually be on my porch. Or that was my plan anyway.

I walked out to the shrub on that afternoon and laid my carrot right next to where I saw his little face. Of course, he scurried away as soon as I got up to walk over, but, after I sat back down (and sat very still), he reappeared and snatched the carrot. I smiled, thinking about him enjoying a free meal in his lair, and got up reluctantly to go back to work rehabbing mine.

Almost every day that summer I laid out a small carrot or other vegetable for the little bunny. And I moved his food a little closer to my porch every time—careful not to overdo it or move too fast, so as not to spook him and ruin the experiment. The food was placed closer in such tiny increments that the little guy probably didn't even notice he was venturing further out to claim his meal each day. And, whenever possible, I sat on my back porch and watched the bunny grab it so he'd associate me with his feasts.

By early August I was excitedly laying the carrot very close to my back porch steps. When I finally moved the meal to the steps, themselves, I could hardly wait to see the bunny complete my goal. On August 22nd, at 3:30 p.m., that little guy finally got up on my back porch and claimed some cherry tomatoes for himself. It took him about three minutes to decide to climb all the way onto the porch, but, by gosh, he was up there. I had achieved my goal—and my furry friend had feasted luxuriously all summer to help me do it.

It took almost three months, but I had slowly but surely changed my little bunny's beliefs about how safe it was for him to approach me and get up on my porch. By moving the food only a tiny bit at a time and making sure he saw me as often as possible (keeping still and silent as he grabbed his treats), he eventually wound up where I planned.

As proud of myself as I was, little did I know that I'd done something even more profound than train a wild animal. I had created a foundational model for how to unlock the law of attraction's greatest potential for influencing our material reality. It was years later that I learned how illustrative my bunny experiment really was. The way I coaxed that bunny to my Keedysville porch is almost exactly how we can best change our beliefs to manifest a more desirable material reality. Coaxing that rabbit is a perfect metaphor and model for how we can manifest our grandest (and most frustratingly absent) desires.

Just as I did with my friend the bunny, I later learned how to lure my subconscious into believing new things that are aligned with some of my greatest desires in a wide array of areas. You, too, will soon learn how to coax your brain into believing just what you need it to so you can finally manifest some of the biggest desires you have. And in this book, I'll not only explain how to do that, but also why you should do it in the exact manner I'm about to teach you.

Your payoff, should you choose to apply yourself to the can't-fail instructions you're about to read, will be the realization of some of your largest and most important dreams. Your grandest desires can come to fruition, in fact. With practice and patience, you will soon have your own "cute little bunny" eating a cherry tomato on your back porch. And I can't wait to see that happen for you.

# Chapter One—What to Expect from This Book and How It Will Help You

This book is intended to provide you with a coach in book form. Since the introduction of my *Why Quantum Physicists...* book series, I've been contacted by many people who say, "Okay, I'm in. I'm sold on your explanations for how I create my material reality through my expectations, and I'm sold on your explanations for how to align my material reality with my desires by improving my beliefs—which automatically improves my expectations. Now, tell me exactly, step-by-step, how to improve my beliefs about (insert a common desire such as health, more money, self-worth, etc.)."

So here it is: your step-by-step instructions for changing any belief to align with your desired outcome. I've intended this book to be conversational in tone and nature. I want it to read like I'm talking to you because I want it to feel like you've got an expert, belief-raising, law of attraction coach sitting in your living room with you. And, with this book, you now do.

What you will find in this book is a necessary overview of your brain (so you know enough about how it works and what its function is), a review of how your beliefs create your reality (so you know why you need to change them), a description of how you got your beliefs in the first place (so you understand how simple it is to change them), a detailed explanation of how to use my process to change your beliefs (so you can finally align them with, and manifest, your desires), additional coaching to help you as you work my process (so you can keep moving forward and align your beliefs with your desires), a description of the first time I used my process (so you have my example to draw upon), and a description of a coaching client's first-time use of my process (so you can see how it worked for someone else). I believe you've got everything you need to manifest your dreams right here in this powerful little book.

You should know that I like to have fun with the process of raising beliefs. I view this process as not only the key to finally living a life of your dreams, but also the most fun and exciting game any human can play.

I call this game "Grow a Greater You," and I'm very excited you're going to start playing it in such a specific and impactful way with me. I don't call it a game, by the way, because it is trivial. To the contrary, "Grow a Greater You" is the most important and rewarding game you, or any human, can play. I call it a game because, quite simply, it's fun.

In my experience, there is nothing more fun than waking up each day and having the opportunity to play "Grow a Greater You." I trust that you, too, will find the fun and excitement in this game—primarily because it works so well. Play the game exactly as you're coached in this book and you will not—you cannot—fail to greatly improve your material reality, aligning your life much more closely with your longest held and dearest desires.

Although I cover the basics of my teachings about how we create our material reality and the role our beliefs (and expectations) play in that process, I do make the assumption that you have read my other books in the *Why Quantum Physicists...* series. If you haven't read them, I'm certain this book can still be of great value to you, yet I also highly recommend that you do read them. It will probably be best to start with *Why Quantum Physicists Do Not Fail* and work your way through the rest. They are all available on Amazon.

You will encounter some repetition in this book. That is done intentionally. As your coach, it is important for me to continually refer back to information that is not only very important but probably new to you. Research indicates that we usually need to hear something three times before we act on it or respond to it. You'll read certain ideas and concepts repeatedly throughout (usually stated a bit differently each time), and I've done that on purpose.

In fact, all of my books follow this concept to a degree—and for exactly the same reasons.

By the way, many have asked me if this book is a law of attraction book. You bet it is. While I didn't title it as such, what you are about to learn will remove most of the obstacles that prevent you from using the law of attraction as you hoped you could when you first encountered it. My books have always been very popular with law of attraction enthusiasts, and I expect this book will probably be my most popular yet—and for very good reasons.

Most people find that the law of attraction allows them to improve their lives and manifest "small" things that make them happy, so they come to believe that the law of attraction is real. These people are correct—it is real. Where most people stall and sputter, however, is with the "big" things they have desired most dearly and for the longest time—financial freedom, a healthy body, having a soul mate, enjoying material abundance, etc.—the things whose absence causes them the most pain. When it comes to those "big" desires, for most people, the law of attraction just doesn't seem to work.

Perhaps you've felt that way yourself. And, perhaps, like many you've assumed the fault was that the law of attraction doesn't really work (or at least not for you) or that you were doing it wrong. Nothing could be further from the truth. The law of attraction is genuine, it does work exactly as you've read (and hoped), and it will work for you as surely as anyone else on Earth.

What you're about to learn, in fact, are the missing set of instructions for using the law of attraction to manifest your greatest desires. No longer do you need to pretend it's okay to not have them or that you really don't want them that much anyway. You may not read the words "law of attraction" throughout the majority of this book, but you can bet the house that you're about to learn everything you need to know to unleash that elusive genie you've always dreamed about. You're about to become a certified law of attraction master practitioner, manifesting your desires in a manner that will astound you and your loved ones.

So, let's begin. Set aside your preconceptions about what all the rules are for being human—you don't need most of them anymore and many of them haven't served you very well anyway. Open your mind to new ideas that come from the most accurate and precise scientific explanations of how our universe works and how you create your material reality. Immerse yourself in my expert coaching. I've done this for years and I "haven't lost one yet"! Follow my instructions to the letter. They are honed through years of experience and trial-and-error. Visit my website if you have questions.

And, most of all, get ready for the ride of your life as you start to play the coolest and most fun and rewarding game you've ever encountered.

# Chapter Two—An Overview of Your Brain's Actual Functionality and Use

The process you're about to learn will actually retrain your brain in ways that will allow you to manifest some of your longest absent, most coveted desires. So let's take a moment to review some important information about your brain. We'll briefly cover how your brain makes decisions, which will help you understand why you need to retrain the subconscious portion of it in the first place. Then we'll cover exactly what your brain's purpose and function are so you can start using it properly—letting it do what it was made to do (and what it does very well) instead of what you always thought it was supposed to do. The truth about your brain may surprise you.

It is now common knowledge that the human brain has three very distinct sections to it—the Neomammalian, the Paleomammalian, and the Reptilian. The two of concern to you are the Neomammalian and the Paleomammalian sections because these two reveal the human decision-making process and how emotions (or feelings) factor into it.

The Reptilian Brain is as primitive as a shark's. It does not consider consequences. If you hold a piece of food in your hand and offer it to a shark, the shark will bite off your hand in addition to the food. The shark, of course, with its Reptilian Brain, does not consider that biting off your hand will end the possible future flow of food.

The Paleomammalian Brain is like a mammal's brain. It does consider consequences but it does not use logic to make decisions—only emotion. If you hold a piece of food in your hand and offer it to a horse, the horse will eat the food but leave your hand. The horse, with its Paleomammalian Brain, understands that biting your hand may result in ending the supply of food.

The Neomammalian Brain is a human adaptation. It uses logic and represents a great difference between us and other animals. If you hold a piece of food in your hand and offer it to a human, the human will not only take the food without biting the hand, she will also use reason to discern exactly how she needs to behave to ensure additional feeding. A human, with her Neomammalian Brain, uses logic to determine behavior that will best guarantee future outcomes.

The Neomammalian Brain, it turns out, uses logic while the Paleomammalian Brain uses emotion. Guess which part of the brain you use to make decisions? The answer may not be what you expect.

(The Paleomammalian Brain, by the way, can also be called your subconscious brain, and that's how I'll be referring to it from here on out.)

So which part of our brain do humans use to make decisions? The Neomammalian part or the subconscious part? While most of us like to think of ourselves as rational, logical people, decades of rigorous research by psychologists such as Dr. Robert Cialdini have proven that humans do not use the logical part of our brains when making decisions. Instead, we use our subconscious, or Paleomammalian, brain almost exclusively to make any decision. The Neomammalian brain is used only after the emotional, subconscious part of our brain has made a decision— and then only to justify the decision the subconscious brain has already made.

The process happens so fast, research shows, that we feel like we're using logic to make our decisions; we truly think we're "enlightened" creatures who differentiate ourselves from the rest of the animal kingdom because we make logical decisions. But we are wrong in that assumption. We are different from almost every other animal because we can, and often do, utilize logic, but we do not utilize it to make decisions as we once believed.

Here is a simple illustration of how emotion and logic are utilized to make a decision:

Why does a woman marry a man? Does a woman marry a man because he is good with a hammer, keeps the car serviced, places his socks in the dirty clothes hamper, and puts the cap back on the toothpaste? No. Those are logical reasons to marry someone. She marries him for one simple reason—because she loves him. A woman's subconscious brain decides that she loves her chosen mate; her decision to marry is truly based on emotion. According to the best research, a woman only uses that logical evidence I listed, concerning what might make a man a good mate, to justify her emotional decision to marry. Those logical reasons are only engaged after she had already decided to marry him based on emotion.

And, of course, men make decisions in the same manner; the same example could be given from a man's point of view.

No matter how true it may be, logic will never engage your subconscious brain and you will never use logic to truly make any decision because your subconscious brain eschews and ignores logic. It only uses emotion. It only cares about emotion. Thus, new emotions (or feelings) are necessary if you want to affect any change upon your subconscious brain.

And guess what part of your brain you will be retraining to build new beliefs that are aligned with, and allow you to manifest, your desires? Yep. Your subconscious brain. Because that is where your beliefs are stored.

I hope these facts about your subconscious brain not only reveal exactly why the process you're about to learn is so necessary, but also motivate you as you work my process to build your new beliefs. Because it is your subconscious brain that you must "trick" into having new beliefs, in order to align your beliefs with your desires and manifest a material reality much more in line with your desires.

Furthermore, what is your brain's true function and role? If you are like most people you have long viewed your brain as "you." But your brain is not who you are. Research has shown very clearly that your brain executes your thoughts and commands but it does not create them. The creation of your thoughts and commands falls exclusively within the domain of the powers of the mind, or consciousness, which is not a physical "object." Your mind, or consciousness, is a non-physical entity; your consciousness cannot be located anywhere in your physical body because it is an energy.

Take note that I am talking about two distinctly different things when I use the terms "brain" and "mind." Your brain is a physical object located inside your skull, an amazing tool that serves you just like your heart, lungs, nervous system, etc. Your mind, however, is a non-physical energy that cannot be found anywhere in your physical form. I use the term "mind" as another word for consciousness, and it can rightfully be called the real "you" because it is the part of you that creates thoughts and gives commands—ones that your physical body, including your brain, executes.

A hundred years of neural research have never located a part of the human brain where commands are given, only where they are executed. That is because there is no part of your brain that can make commands.

What are the consequences of operating under the illusion that your brain is who you are—that your brain is your "commander"? The direst one is this: You almost always define yourself by your circumstances, and this has been a big part of what's kept you apart from your greatest desires. When you harbor the illusion of brain as commander, you adopt a state of being (who you are) based upon your current circumstances.

In other words, because you see empty bank accounts, you believe, "I am not wealthy." Because you see sickness, you believe, "I am not healthy." Because you see a job with long hours, lots of stress, and low pay, you believe, "I do not have a good job."

This is backwards. This is incorrect. This paradigm, caused by the illusion that your brain is who you are, is akin to taking a bus ride and believing, "I own a bus and I always travel in it" just because you happen to be sitting in one. Wouldn't you call such a belief "wacko"? Yet you enact such a wacko belief until you learn that your brain does not have the power or capability to create commands—it can only execute them.

Among its many functions, your brain is a complex physical warehouse that stores your beliefs (in the subconscious part of it). It also executes all your commands (which are made by your mind). Your brain does not, technically, create your material reality; your reality merely reflects your beliefs and the expectations that arise from them. What you are seeing in your current reality is simply the result of your previous beliefs and expectations. You should never define your state of being (who you are) based upon the result of your previous beliefs and expectations (which is your current reality).

Your previous beliefs and expectations have no bearing on your future manifestations *unless you let them*.

Yet that is what you are doing every day if you let your brain be your "commander." The brain has no power to give commands. The brain's power is limited to carrying out commands. That is what it is made to do, that is what it is good at doing, and that is what you should limit it to doing. Fortunately, this is exactly what you will be retraining your brain to do as you work this process to build new beliefs. You'll be stripping it, in ways that really work, of its role as the "commander" of who you are and using it properly as a great ally that is an expert at carrying out the commands that the real you, your consciousness, gives it.

The powers of your mind, however, are unlimited. Your mind, or consciousness, decides your thoughts, decisions, and actions. It is your "commander." The powers of your mind are the powers you've always been seeking. The power to manifest anything you desire comes from the powers of your mind.

Your brain has had years of free reign. It feels entitled to its longstanding role as your "commander," and the rest of your body has accepted its kingship as the norm. But you will learn, in this book, exactly how to engage the incredible power of your mind, as well as your subconscious brain, and build the new beliefs you need to align your life with your desires.

# Chapter Three—How Your Beliefs Create Your Material Reality

Now let's take a moment to review how you create your material reality. As you will see, your brain does play an important role but perhaps not the one you once imagined.

Of seminal importance for you is understanding that nothing in the material universe is a preexisting entity. No material object exists independent of you, awaiting your discovery. You are, literally, the creator of all that you see and experience. There is an ancient philosophical query that goes, "If a tree falls in the forest and no one is there, does it make a sound?" The answer to this question is that if there is no one there, there is no forest at all. The material world is actually a comingling of your energy (your consciousness or the real "you") with the energy of the quantum field from whence the material world is manifest.

The quantum field, by the way, is an unbound, unformed field of energy representing the possibility to become anything. It is an infinite ocean of energy that waits in a state of pure potential to be commanded to take concrete form—forming "things" and creating your material reality.

Physicists refer to the process of creating your material world as "collapsing the quantum possibility wave," because they have come to understand that all subatomic particles (the tiny portions of the quantum field) exist in a state of mere potential until human attention is placed upon them. You collapse the quantum possibility wave any time you awaken your senses and observe, which is an act that commands subatomic particles to abandon their state of potential and respond to your expectations in forming material objects. This process of creation is exactly why we can call this process a comingling of your innate energy with the quantum field from whence material objects emerge. Material objects are created solely in context with you.

Thus, we now know that the creation of the material world is not a bottom-up process as your naked eyes lead you to believe. Instead, the creation of the material world is a top-down process. And it is your observations and, more precisely, your expectations that command the unformed field of energy to manifest into concrete, distinct material objects.

Let's next look at where your expectations come from. Your expectations are derived unconsciously from your beliefs; what you believe will always dictate what you expect. Your expectations (which continually command the field of energy to manifest into physical reality) are created by what you believe.

What can be frustrating for you is that the quantum field does not care whether your beliefs align with your conscious desires. The quantum field will deliver unwanted things just as reliably as desired ones (I'll explain this, and how to rectify the problem, in greater detail later). The quantum field doesn't care if a physical manifestation is experienced by you as "good" or "bad," only that it matches up with your expectations.

The next logical piece for you to understand is where your beliefs come from. While a belief carries with it the overwhelming feeling of being "correct," you must understand that any belief you hold is correct only for you. A belief is not independently correct, nor should it be assumed to universally apply to everyone (or anyone) else. Why not? Because a belief is nothing more than something you have told yourself for so long that it has assumed that mantle for you and you alone.

You intuitively know that there are many things you label "good" or "bad," while other people choose to label them the opposite— from seemingly trivial things such as foods, hairstyles, cell phone plans, or soft drinks to things that may have much more importance to you, such as religion, political parties, career choices, and military conflicts. And while it might be silly to suggest that you should never form such judgments about things in your life, it is most certainly true that your judgments are always subjective, unique to you, personal, and optional.

There is no event or circumstance in your life that negates your option of making your own personal choice about how to label it. Certainly there are things that are more challenging *not* to label "good" (such as winning the lottery) or "bad" (such as being diagnosed with cancer), but we've all read about a lottery winner who was bankrupt within a couple of years (and in worse financial shape than before the lottery win) and the cancer patient who overcame her diagnosis (teaching and inspiring many people in the process). What those examples clearly illustrate is that nothing, no matter how completely and totally "good" or "bad" it seems, is ever *independently* or *universally* "good" or "bad." You always retain the choice to label your life's events and circumstances however you decide.

I hope, by now, you can see what a powerful creator you are. You have, in fact, been creating your material reality in this manner since childhood. You will soon be using this information to motivate your no-holds-barred immersion in the process you're about to learn. And you will become a much more powerful and influential creator of your material reality. To recap what quantum physics tells us about how you create your material reality:

1. The material world is created by you through your expectations for it.

2. Your expectations are created, unconsciously, by your beliefs.

3. Your beliefs are your most practiced, habitual thoughts. They are subjective and true for you, alone, because you have made them so.

4. You can change any belief you choose if you want to align a belief with a desire you have.

5. If you change a belief, the expectations it unconsciously creates will naturally change too.

6. Once your expectations change, your material reality will change in accordance. This is how our universe functions; you can depend on that.

We are now full-circle back to the secret I revealed earlier. If you wish to create and experience a physical reality much more closely aligned with your desires, you now know exactly what to do. The list above spells it out in sequential fashion. And the one actionable item from that list? The one, most important, piece of work you must do? Perhaps the only work you must do? Of course: Change your beliefs.

Isn't that great news? If you want to see and experience a material reality more in line with your conscious dreams and desires, all you need to do is change your beliefs. And you can be assured that, when you focus on deliberate creation in this manner, you are following the blueprint for how our universe really works: the blueprint given to us by quantum physics, the most accurate and reliable science ever created.

I spent the first 40 years of my life thinking that my thoughts were reactions to my life experiences. Funny. Good to know, now, that it's the other way around.

Through quantum physics we can now say that everything we experience is self-referral. Everything in our material world is all the same thing, created from the quantum field. Seen in this way, we can say that your life is all simply you experiencing yourself.

You've heard it said that this is all an illusion? That's true, but there is an important distinction to understand. "All is illusion..." doesn't refer to all material objects in the universe being "not real." They're real, all right.

No, the illusion referred to by "All is illusion..." is that we are separate from all physical objects in our material reality. The illusion is that I think there is a separate entity called "Greg" who is a unique and separate "thing" that's distinct from my wife, sons, alarm clock, nightstand, etc.

The illusion is that I'm not simply interacting with myself, since I am creating everything I experience through my expectations. That's what "all is self-referral" means. Everything in the universe is really the self observing the self.

You can experience this for yourself through meditation and entering what some call "the gap." When you are in the gap, you experience timeless awareness. Timeless awareness is where the observer, the observed, and the act of observation become one. During timeless awareness all possibilities are present, because you are actually in commune with the quantum field.

This is why it is important for you (eventually) to hold beliefs of love/joy/appreciation in all areas, because true love/joy/ appreciation is one of the best ways to experience timeless awareness. When you hold those beliefs, you lose the illusion of being separated from your object of love/joy/appreciation. Think about times when you were spellbound by gratitude, love, or appreciation, such as seeing your child born or watching a spectacular sunset. You lose yourself in those moments; you become one with the "thing" you are observing and forget to think you are separate from it.

When you no longer look at the object or skill you desire to manifest as an "object" to be attained, used, and from which to gratify and/or satisfy yourself, you are in a place of love/joy/ appreciation. You have entered the field of all possibilities. You are no longer something separate from that which you are observing, and your desires can be, literally, spontaneously manifest.

And then, because you're a human being playing this beautiful game called "Grow a Greater You," you will lose that perspective and return to the pain of the illusion. The illusion that you are separate from all other "things." Like me, you're human, and, even after immersing yourself in the process you're about to learn, you'll occasionally go back to the illusion that your spouse, children, alarm clock, nightstand, etc., are not really you in a form of self-referral.

But thanks to this process of building the new beliefs you need so that they are now aligned with your desires, you will continually be able to return to the gap, to timeless awareness. You will experience, more and more, the manifestation of your desires. And you'll find yourself spending more and more time in the gap as the days pass.

By the way, most humans (me included) have made the mistake of thinking that affirmations and positive thinking can supersede negative beliefs. As you have undoubtedly experienced, we quickly find out that is wrong. Positive thinking and affirmations (beautiful tools when used properly) are most often nothing but a thin veneer covering an ocean of negative belief. As they are commonly taught in our culture, they are mostly "smiley faces" slapped over an empty gas gauge.

What you're about to learn is not another spin on positive affirmations, nor is it merely another directive to have positive thought. Those good ideas will never retrain your brain the way you need to. You will enter, instead, into a new realm of conscious connection with the quantum field, which will most likely make your previous use of those tools seem like child's play.

# Chapter Four—How You Acquired Your Beliefs and Why Your Subconscious Brain is Like a Scared Bunny

The process you're learning in this book will systematically retrain your subconscious brain, which, up to this point in your life, has been trained by other people. Your parents, their rules for living, and what they believed were the primary contributors to your brain's training. Your schooling, particularly your early education, was also a huge component. If you were taken to church or had religion as a child, those beliefs, too, undoubtedly had a profound effect upon your brain. Alternatively, the media you were exposed to a child (the books, magazines, television, movies, music, and, if you're young enough, websites) no doubt also greatly influenced and trained your brain.

What does it mean to train, or retrain, your brain? The answer to that question is found in how you build your beliefs. A belief is little more than a thought you've repeated so often that it becomes a dominant neural pathway. Physically, a thought is simply a firing of electricity along a pathway of neurons in your brain. Think the same thought often enough and that pathway becomes dominant and assumes a leading role for you, not only because of its familiarity, but also because you become supremely accustomed to using that neural pathway.

Over the course of time, that practiced neural pathway assumes the mantle of a belief. And, of course, a belief is a truth you hold about life. Thus, with each belief you build, you train your brain. You create a "rulebook" for life—how life works, what you should do, how you should behave, what you should expect, and why things happen the way they do.

We call it "training" your brain because the only way to create a belief is to practice the thought over and over. Building a belief is very much like training a dog. Just as it's the repetition and consistency that solidifies the desired behavior in a dog, so too is it the repetition and consistency that solidifies the behavior (or, the belief) in your brain.

Notice that I omitted the word "desired" in the second half of the previous sentence. I did that on purpose because not all of your beliefs are desirable—at least not in your adult life. Some, or perhaps many, of your beliefs are, in fact, directly opposed to the achievement or manifestation of your desires.

Why? When you were a child, you were not only at your most impressionable but your brain was also very much a blank slate. Your child-brain was like a sponge, readily and hungrily soaking up the beliefs of your parents, teachers, church, and popular media. You absorbed virtually every belief you were exposed to and created your deepest, most powerful beliefs, which you carried into adulthood.

You assimilated the overt lessons and teachings (what your influencers told you and showed you) and, perhaps more importantly, adopted their covert lessons and teachings from how your influencers behaved and what they did. Remember the old command "Do as I say, not as I do"? You learned from what your influencers said, but what they did cemented even more beliefs into the rulebook you built in your brain. Actions, indeed, speak louder than words.

Another reason you absorbed and adopted beliefs so completely during childhood is that you had so much unreserved trust in the sources of those beliefs. You did not yet have the filters of cynicism and jadedness to "protect" you from new ideas; you viewed your parents, and the other sources of beliefs to which they exposed you, as the end-all, be-all of life knowledge.

It is correct to label a child a belief-building organism. You were a blank slate, you were in need of (and eagerly sought out) beliefs, and you were under the unfiltered influence of your parents (and other sources) who transferred beliefs to you with almost God-like authority. And you learned well.

In most cases, the sources of your beliefs did their best to expose you to helpful, beneficial ones. And I'm sure that many of the beliefs you hold as an adult do serve you well. Your parents (and the other sources of your childhood beliefs) were only human, however, and were, like all humans, flawed and influenced by fear. Therefore, some of what they taught you was designed to protect you and save you from pain. Unfortunately, a lot of those types of beliefs have wound up limiting you during your adult life and sometimes even harming you. Examples of this type of belief are teaching a child that she has to be physically beautiful to earn someone's love and respect, or teaching a child that life is full of disappointment, so the sooner he resigns himself to the fact that he shouldn't really expect to have his desires fulfilled in the manner he hopes, the less pain he'll have.

Additionally, as flawed human beings, your childhood sources of beliefs also transferred some to you that are unnecessary or even flat out wrong. Once again, in most cases this wasn't done intentionally. Your sources were operating with the best information they had at the time and that was all they knew how to teach you. These beliefs have also, unfortunately, wound up limiting you as an adult, and even hurting you in some circumstances. Examples of this type of belief include teaching a child that life happens "to" her and she has very little influence over her material reality, or teaching a child that his thoughts and feelings are a result of his life experiences rather than other way around.

Unfortunately there is an even more insidious and harmful type of belief that was undoubtedly transferred to you as a child. In most cases, this type of belief was not given to you to intention-ally harm you (even though it most likely has, to an extent). The sources of your childhood beliefs, as flawed human beings, were also self-focused, and some of what they taught you came from a desire to please themselves or further their own desires. Most guilty of transferring these types of beliefs were the popular media, but other sources (such as ever present and all pervasive advertising) were almost as apt to do likewise. These beliefs carried into adulthood can be some of the more damaging to you, as well as the most immediately recognized as harmful. Examples of these types of beliefs include teaching a child that she needs to consume the latest clothing style to be popular (and, additionally, that being popular should be very important to her) or teaching a child that he is not allowed to get angry because his parents are bothered by it.

Even if you did not recognize any beliefs you currently have from the examples given in the previous three paragraphs, I'm sure it's easy for you to recognize the truth in them. Yet there is still one more important piece of information necessary for you to understand before you begin the process you'll learn in this book: Most adults live their lives as if their beliefs (most of which were given to them during their childhood by, of course, flawed humans) are written in stone—unchangeable and unyielding. Most adults tell themselves some version of "This is just the way life is" regarding their beliefs. And what they are really saying to themselves is, "I don't have any alternative to these beliefs about life because these beliefs are the truth and they are reality." Most adults, of course, tell themselves this even when (or, perhaps, *especially* when) their beliefs are keeping them apart from their desires—when their beliefs are, thus, painful or even harmful.

Beliefs, after all, serve as your internal "rulebook." They tell you how things are, how things are supposed to happen, and how life works. Yet precious few people stop to consider that their internal "rulebook" was created long ago, during their childhood, by people and sources who were flawed and scarred by fear and self-serving behavior. Thus, they never consider that much of their internal "rulebook" is unintentionally limiting and often keeps their greatest desires at arm's length throughout their lives.

Knowing what you now do about how you create your material reality, does an internal "rulebook" created under such influence sound like a recipe for an adult life imbued with abundance in all areas? Does it sound like a formula destined to guarantee an adult the ability to manifest all of her greatest desires? For some people fortunate enough to be raised in an environment of enlightened beliefs, this may be so. But for the vast majority of adults, that old "rulebook" that was created during their childhood is chock full of limiting, fear-based beliefs that create absence, lack, and frustration.

Yet the great news for you, as a now fully aware adult, is that you can change any part of your internal "rulebook" that is not serving you well. Why is that such great news? Refer to what you have already learned through my other books and to what you were reminded of in the previous chapter: Your desires manifest when your beliefs are in alignment with them. And, conversely, most of the pain in your life comes from your beliefs not being in alignment with your desires. In fact, the degree of pain you feel is directly commensurate with the size of the divide between your beliefs and your desires.

Your beliefs are most definitely not the unyielding, carved-in-stone monuments of truth you probably always assumed. They are nothing more than your most practiced thoughts, your dominant neural pathways, inspired (or actually created, in most cases) by trusted sources from your childhood. This means that you, as an adult, have the inherent freedom to change any belief you wish today. And, thanks to this book, you also now possess the ability to do so.

Why would you want to change a belief? Why would you want to change your truth, your internal "rulebook"? The reason you would want to change a belief is simple: Your beliefs always, and without fail, subconsciously create your expectations. And your true expectations, arising automatically from your true beliefs (not, by the way, your top-of-mind wishes and hopes) are the commands you send to the quantum field, telling it how to form your specific material reality—your unique universe. So, unless you enjoy the pain of some of your longest held, most important desires remaining unfulfilled, you will want to change your beliefs pertaining to those desires. It is the only way to consistently exert your positive influence upon your life circumstances.

When should you change a belief? When should you go through the somewhat unsettling experience of jettisoning a long-held truth and adopt a new one? Any time you have the repeated experience of the absence of an important desire. Any time you've experienced pain on a regular basis because you have been unable to achieve, realize, or manifest something very important and highly desired by you. And any time you've found yourself justifying or rationalizing the absence of that important desire—telling yourself some version of "I'm okay without that"; "People who achieve that are shallow or morally suspect"; "Having that thing I desire must be for other people but not for me"; or "I must not be worthy of having that."

How do you change a belief? How do you go into your internal "rulebook," find beliefs that are keeping your desires from manifesting in your material reality, and change them? Well, my friend, you're about to find out exactly how to do that. It's a lot simpler than you might imagine—and you can begin today. Best of all, you'll soon find that, as soon as you begin, your life experiences will start to align with your desires (in small ways at first) almost immediately.

# Chapter Five—My Process to Retrain Your Subconscious Brain and Build New Beliefs that Align With and Manifest Your Desires

This chapter begins with an Emotional Reference Chart. This chart will be necessary to work this process and will guide you as you improve your beliefs as thoroughly as necessary to manifest even your longest held, yet most absent, desires. The terms I selected to label emotions on this chart are not necessarily written in stone. Although I encourage you to use the chart and the emotions I have chosen just as they are written, you may find that other terms and other emotions are more suitable for your journey. If that's the case, don't feel like you're doing anything wrong to substitute a different word or term along the way.

You may benefit from copying this chart and having it at your fingertips. If so, please feel free to visit the Resources page on my website to find a clean copy you can print for yourself. The chart is designed to guide you up a scale of emotions, so you have concrete direction as you build the new beliefs that will align you with any desire you have. You'll notice that it is written in ascending order, with the most negative emotions on the bottom. As you follow the emotions up the chart, eventually ending with the highest emotional state possible, you'll see that they become gradually more positive and more empowering.

The idea of an Emotional Reference Chart, by the way, is inspired by the writings of Jerry and Esther Hicks. I first encountered such a guide in their wonderful book, *Ask and It is Given: Learning to Manifest Your Desires*, and they are responsible for inspiring me to create the following chart.

An Emotional Reference Chart

1. Love/Ecstasy
2. Joy/Elation
3. Ease/Power
4. Confidence/Inspiration
5. Excitement/Passion
6. Anticipation/Eagerness
7. Enthusiasm/Ambition
8. Hopefulness/Optimism
9. Interest/Inquisitiveness
10. Acceptance/Peace
11. Introspection/Contemplation
12. Pensiveness/Melancholy
13. Indifference/Apathy
14. Unease/Discontent
15. Frustration/Aggravation
16. Worry/Nervousness
17. Doubt/Pessimism
18. Anger/Blame
19. Anxiety/Fear
20. Grief/Desolation
21. Despair/Worthlessness
22. Powerlessness/Dejection
23. Depression/Hopelessness

Now you are ready to begin. The process you're about to learn is not complicated, yet I caution you to adhere to the instructions exactly as written. Bear in mind that you will be changing beliefs that are as familiar to you as your favorite pair of blue jeans—and just as easy to slip into. Even though the beliefs you are changing are undoubtedly painful, do not underestimate the siren call of familiar pain. Familiar pain is predictable and reliable. It is "a known commodity" and thus is preferable to your subconscious brain (the "scared bunny").

This fact is voiced in the old saying "Better the devil you know." We all share a common pull from our subconscious to stick with what we've previously experienced because that is the "safest" option. As you've learned, in order for you to create new expectations that will command the quantum field to manifest your desires, your subconscious brain must be led into new beliefs that are aligned with your desires.

Doing something new, even with the promise of freedom behind it, is unfamiliar and unknown; hence, your subconscious will not jump on board and happily spur you forward. Knowing this, it is important to not only follow the instructions for how to write about your emotions, but also to stick to the timeframe I provide you. Changing beliefs is a scary thing to your unconscious. Remember the little bunny in the bushes? You must slowly and gradually lure your subconscious into the new beliefs. In fact, it's not incorrect to say that you'll be "tricking" your subconscious brain into holding the new beliefs.

Another thing before you begin. You'll find me using the terms "beliefs", "emotional perspectives", and "feelings" interchangeably. In almost every instance during this process, those words mean just about the same thing, because your emotional perspectives and feelings reveal your beliefs. Additionally, creating new feelings about something creates new beliefs. So when you change your feelings you automatically change your beliefs. The two are that intertwined and, for our purposes, can be used interchangeably.

Ready? Here is the process. Please don't be fooled by how simple it may sound at first read.

1. Using the Emotional Reference Chart, identify how you feel about the thing you desire that is currently absent from your life.

2. Select the next highest emotion up the chart and write about your absent desire from that perspective.

3. Live your way into that next highest emotion over the course of one to three days (or longer if you feel it necessary).

4. Select the next highest emotion up the chart from the one you just wrote about/lived your way into and write about it/live your way into it in the same manner you did with the previous one.

5. Never moving more than one emotion up at a time and never more than one emotion up per day, repeat steps 2 through 4 until you have moved yourself all the way up to the top of the Emotional Reference Chart.

Now let's examine each of these steps in detail to ensure you're ready to work this process completely and manifest any desire you have. As I describe each step, I'll write about it with examples from my real-life use of this process.

## Step One: Identify How You Currently Feel About Your Chosen Absent Desire

You begin this process by identifying an issue or topic about which you are experiencing pain. You're experiencing pain, of course, because you don't have what you desire—you haven't been able to manifest it. This will be an issue about which your material reality has consistently been falling very short of your desires. Remember that almost all emotional pain is the result of the distance between your beliefs and your desires. The greater the distance, the greater the pain.

The first desire I ever used this process to raise my beliefs on was "financial abundance" (or "having more money"), so I'll use it to illustrate these steps for you. Of course, you should follow the same steps I'm outlining here for any topic or issue of your choosing, such as self-worth, having a soul mate, career, weight, health, parenting, relationships, etc.

Simply take out a piece of paper and a pen (I like to use a journal since that keeps a record of all my writing in one place) and write about your true feelings regarding the desire you have chosen to raise your beliefs on. Let yourself freely write anything that wants to come out. Nothing is out of bounds or off-limits; however, stick to what you are really feeling about it—not how you *want* to feel about it or how you think you *ought* to feel about it.

Give yourself an honest assessment regarding how you feel about your absent desire. In my example, I asked myself, "What are my real, gut-level feelings around money?"—not "Where would I like them to be?" but "What are they, really?" We're not used to telling it like it is to ourselves, because it's painful to do so.

(These feelings are not going to be positive and they will not feel good either. Get past your wishful thinking about your absent desire and dismiss how you think you "ought" to feel about it to manifest it. It takes courage to write honestly here, because these feelings are no fun to think about and deal with. But remember: If your true feelings—and, thus, your true beliefs— about your absent desire were positive, you'd already be manifesting it.)

So you need to write and write and write—until you've feel like you've emptied your gut of all the negative, scary, bad-feeling stuff in there. In my example of financial abundance, I wrote things like:

"I hate that I never have enough money."

"Money is scarce and there's never enough."

"I never get ahead. When I do catch a break and get more money (an income tax refund, for example), it always disappears quickly and I never get to use it like I really want to."

"People who have lots of money are greedy."

"Money is the root of all evil."

"It's shallow and wrong to want more money than I need."

"Financial abundance is something that happens for other people, lucky people, but not for me."

"People do bad things to get more money than they need."

Here's something important that might help you have the courage to write honestly about your absent desire. You will not write down anything, no matter how negative it is, that you're not already dealing with every day, at least on an unconscious level. In other words, writing about these bad feelings doesn't "make them real." They are already real—you're just admitting them openly and honestly through your writing. It's only scary because you're undoubtedly not in the habit of honestly looking them square in the face every day. Who would want to do that (until now, of course)?

Let's get honest here. When it comes to what has been up to now your difficult-to-manifest, deeply yearned for yet absent desires, it's much more comfortable to slap a smiley face over an empty gas gauge then it is to go fill the gas tank. Your empty gas gauge is your absent desire, which is painful to experience. And the smiley face is your natural human tendency to tell yourself that you don't really want your desire—to rationalize its absence or deny the pain of its absence. Of course, you would never do this with your car, in real life, because you know you'd run out of gas and be stranded somewhere away from home. But, if you're like most people, you've been doing it all the time to yourself spiritually as you slap smiley faces over your bad feelings. And, since you've undoubtedly been in a habit of doing this with the desire you're writing about, it's natural to feel some inertia when you begin this initial writing.

So you'll need to officially declare, "No more smiley faces on my painfully absent desire." In my example, I certainly didn't feel good about financial abundance. I hated that I didn't have the amount of money I desired. It sucked to want more money and not have it.

After you finish emotionally vomiting your real, honest, painful, current feelings about your absent desire through your writing, look on the Emotional Reference Chart and identify where you currently are. In my case I saw that my writing aligned me most closely with Powerlessness/Dejection because I was consumed with the belief that I was never going to see more money and that I'd always want more than I had despite all my deep desires and previous hard work to attain it. I was dejected because all my previous efforts had been wasted and it seemed I didn't deserve more money—no matter how much I wanted it.

Whenever I use this process to raise my beliefs about any desire I've been out of alignment with, I have always found myself at the one of the low emotional perspectives. Since you are using this technique to address a desire that you haven't been manifesting in accordance with your beliefs, you're obviously going to find yourself rather low on the emotional chart as well.

At this point, write the name of the next highest emotion from the reference chart. I wrote "Next Time—Despair/Worthlessness" at the bottom because "Despair/Worthlessness" is the next highest emotion on the Emotional Reference Chart from the initial emotion I identified with.

## Step Two: Select the Next Highest Emotion Up the Chart and Write About Your Absent Desire from that Perspective

When you're ready to begin moving up the chart (ideally the very next day), get out your journal and write about your absent desire from the perspective of the next highest emotion on the reference chart (the emotion you wrote "Next Time" by). Look up the dictionary definition of that emotion because that helps clarify the emotion you'll be writing about (and seeking to live yourself into).

Once you know the definition of that next highest emotion, sit down and write about your absent desire from the perspective of that emotion. The way you move into a new emotional perspective of your desire is to write in freeform how that desire will look/feel/sound/taste/smell/etc. from that new perspective. Write in the present tense: Instead of writing about how it *would* feel, write about how it *does* feel. While you write, once again give yourself permission to really feel that emotion regarding your absent desire. Contemplate your absent desire from the perspective of this new emotion. Mentally roll around in this new emotion, set up camp in it, and write about it until you've emptied yourself out.

In my example, I learned that "Despair" meant "to lose all hope or confidence" and "Worthlessness" means "useless and contemptible."

So my next writing contained new thoughts and feelings like:

"I have no hope that I'll ever have more money."

"It's hopeless for me to think that I'll ever achieve my desires for money. Just look at my track record."

"My confidence level is near zero regarding my ability to have the money that I really desire."

"I have no confidence in the universe. I've been denied my desire for more money my entire life."

"I feel useless because I'm always one step behind, always in debt, and can't provide myself or my family with the life I want because I never have the money I want and need."

"It's useless to try. I'm obviously not worthy of the money I truly desire."

"People experiencing financial abundance are cor
because it's not fair that they get to have something ⅃
badly but can never attain."

"I feel contempt for the universe because I work and try hard
and desire money greatly but never have what I want."

Notice that I took great care to write about financial abundance
from this new emotional perspective—and that it's purposely
not radically different from the previous perspective. Remember: You must take small steps to build new beliefs, because the
"scared bunny" (your subconscious brain) will not believe or
accept anything but small, positive increments in your beliefs.

When you feel you've written everything you can and your gut
feels empty, write the name of the next highest emotion on the
reference chart at the bottom of the writing you just completed. I
wrote "Next Time—Grief/Desolation" at the bottom because
"Grief/Desolation" was the next highest emotion on the
Emotional Reference Chart from the emotion I just wrote about.

By the way, these new perspectives won't feel much more
positive than the previous ones, and that, too, is intentional. But
each emotion is a little more positive, and I believe you'll see that
reflected in your writing—even though the uptick of positivity is
relatively minor. This will hold true each time you move one tick
up the emotional perspective chart.

## Step Three: Live Your Way into that Next Highest Emotion Over the Course of One to Three Days (or Longer if You Feel it Necessary)

Next, make it your job to see your absent desire from the
perspective of the emotion you just wrote about. Think about it
from that perspective, meditate about it, and let it ruminate in
your mind. Throughout your normal daily affairs, roll around in
the perspective of that new emotion like a dog in newly mown
grass. Embrace that new emotional perspective, pain and all,

with full-on honesty regarding your absent desire. No justification. No rationalization. No wishful thinking.

One of the most powerful tools for living your way into this new emotion is to tell new stories about your desire from that emotional perspective. This is a process I focus on teaching you in my books and on my website.

Here is a review of how and why you should tell new stories. You intuitively know that there are many things you label "good" or "bad," while other people choose to label them the opposite—from seemingly trivial things such as foods, hairstyles, cell phone plans, or soft drinks to things that may have much more importance to you, such as religion, political parties, career choices, and military conflicts. And while it might be silly to suggest that you should never form such judgments about things in your life, it *is* most certainly true that your judgments are always subjective, unique to you, personal, and optional.

There is no event or circumstance in your life that negates your option of making your own personal choice about how to label it. Certainly there are things that are more challenging *not* to label "good" (such as winning the lottery) or "bad" (such as being diagnosed with cancer), but we've all read about a lottery winner who was bankrupt within a couple of years (and in worse financial shape than before the lottery win) and the cancer patient who overcame her diagnosis (teaching and inspiring many people in the process). What those examples clearly illustrate is that nothing, no matter how completely and totally "good" or "bad" it seems, is ever *independently* or *universally* "good" or "bad." You always retain the choice to label your life's events and circumstances however you decide.

Your stories about your life events and circumstances are, therefore, subjective. What you have undoubtedly called "telling it like it is" has always actually been "telling it as you're choosing to tell it." It matters not that everyone else also tells the same stories about any event or circumstance; the decision to call something "good" or "bad" has always been, and will always be, your choice. I am not suggesting that you should be able to call something unwanted "good", nor am I recommending that you no longer affirm your true feelings about things. What I am telling you, however, is that there is no law which states you must always define the value of your life events and circumstances from a negative, or guarded, perspective. You can choose to start telling better-feeling stories, which are still believable, about any event or circumstance in your life.

Eventually you will be able to tell amazingly positive stories about your desires and almost any circumstance, but those types of stories won't be effective at first because you won't really believe them. Your beliefs and your desires are simply too far out of alignment currently for this kind of abrupt 180-degree change in your storytelling to be real for you. So the best method to use when you first start telling new, better stories, is to consciously preface it with, "I currently believe (or feel)" and to follow it with, "But I believe that, with practiced effort, I can learn to tell better stories about (that thing or event) over the course of time." You might also add, "And if I consciously choose to tell better stories about (that thing or event), I believe that, over time, my beliefs will change about it and, thus, so will my material reality and experiences concerning it."

With continued practice, you will find that by prefacing and following up your statements as prescribed, you will begin to see new possibilities. You will notice a new freedom to think about your life experiences in fresh, more positive ways and, thus, feel inspired to tell even better stories more readily. Use this freedom to experiment and play with the new, better stories you're telling about your life experiences. You may feel inspired to tell better stories about undesirable outcomes or circumstances such as "Perhaps this is happening just like it's supposed to, although I may lack the perspective to understand why right now" or "Maybe this experience is just what I need, although it might not seem to be from my current perspective" or "Although this is not what I desired, I can believe that this outcome is an improvement over my previous experiences, and I can believe that further improvements are possible if I keep practicing the three steps of this process Greg has taught me." Whether you tell yourself these stories or others unique to you, you will find that they become self-fulfilling prophecies, bringing incrementally better experiences into your material reality.

You should also let yourself be inspired to create games and activities to keep you focused on your alignment with your desire. In Chapter Seven, I'll give you examples of games and activities I created and used during my own process.

In reasonably short order, you'll be able to truly see your absent desire from the perspective of that new emotion. That is because that new emotion is really not that much more positive than the previous one. By the next day (or two or three days later—however long it takes you), you'll feel like you've gotten a handle on your absent desire from the perspective of the new emotion.

I took care to keep the focus on Despair/Worthlessness and not on the feelings I wrote about previously. When I found myself drifting back to the feelings I had previously written about, I simply gently reminded myself to focus, instead, on Despair/Worthlessness. These were believable reminders since I wasn't asking myself to adopt new feelings that were way up the chart. The perspective of Despair/Worthlessness is, after all, only slightly more positive than my previous emotional perspective.

I found that, with that much effort and attention, I was able to really make an actual transition from Powerlessness/Dejection to Despair/Worthlessness regarding financial abundance. The transition started when I first looked up the definitions, catapulted forward when I wrote about financial abundance from the perspective of Despair/Worthlessness, and solidified as I began to focus on financial abundance from the perspective of Despair/Worthlessness during my normal, daily affairs. I was really there. I was then feeling completely desperate and worthless about financial abundance.

Here's how a literal transition to the new emotional perspective (not just a fanciful "what if") is possible. It's not that big of a leap. It's a realistic uptick of emotional perspective. It feels real and genuine because it's only a slight improvement—not a smiley face slapped over an empty gas gauge. It's believable, and my subconscious brain will accept it because it's not some grandiose "quantum leap" way up the chart (like a positive affirmation attempts to do for you). Additionally, I undoubtedly was familiar with feeling Despair/Worthlessness about financial abundance anyway.

Sometimes it takes a couple of days to really embrace the next highest emotion—and that's fine. It takes as long as it takes. But I don't intentionally procrastinate on the process. I think about it, meditate about it, and write more about it (if necessary) until I have become that emotional perspective.

## Step Four: Select the Next Highest Emotion Up the Chart From the One You Just Wrote About/Lived Your Way Into and Write About It/Live Your Way Into It in the Same Manner You Did with the Previous One

You've lived your way, in slow, realistic, believable fashion, into a slightly higher emotional perspective than the one you held previously. You wrote, "Next Time" and included the next highest emotion from the emotional perspective chart at the end of your previous writing. Now it's simply time to get your journal back out and repeat the process with the next, slightly higher emotional perspective from the chart. Do the same things you did previously: Write about your absent desire from the new emotional perspective and then spend a day or two (or three—however long it takes) living your way into that new perspective from that new emotion.

In my example, I next wrote about financial abundance from the perspective of Grief/Desolation, and my writing was aimed purely at seeing financial abundance from that emotion. As I had found previously, Grief/Desolation was a relatively easy perspective to attain as it was not that much more positive than Despair/Worthlessness and, as before, these were feelings I had some familiarity with. And, once again, I found that the new feelings and perspectives were only slightly more positive than the previous ones—not radically so.

## Step Five: Never Moving More than One Emotion Up at a Time and Never Moving More than One Emotion Up Per Day, Repeat Steps 2 through 4 Until You Have Moved Yourself All the Way Up to the Top of the Emotional Reference Chart

Each new emotional perspective builds new neural pathways in your brain; thus, it builds new beliefs. In following this process as instructed, you are retraining your brain—throwing out portions of that old childhood rulebook and replacing them with new beliefs that serve you because they are more aligned with your desires.

It is very important to move only one emotion at a time. And move, at most, only one emotion per day (no matter how "on fire" you are to live your way into the new emotional perspective and how completely and authentically you do that). Moving at a pace any faster is like slapping a smiley face on an empty gas gauge. Always remember: No matter how greatly you wish to finally manifest your long absent desire, you are coaxing a scared little bunny out of the bushes, asking her to take a carrot from your hand. That bunny (your subconscious brain) will only move toward you in small, safe, believable increments.

But don't fret about the seemingly slow pace of this process. As you move up the chart, you'll notice that what you're manifesting regarding your desire improves almost immediately. Sure, the improvements are not dramatic at first. In the beginning, you're still at emotional perspectives that are usually far from being aligned with your desires. But, even in the beginning, you will be improving your beliefs slightly, and that will send new commands to the quantum field (even though your commands will, obviously, not manifest your desire in the grand manner they eventually will). That's because your beliefs (and, thus, your unconscious expectations, which send new commands to the quantum field) are different with even a single tick up the chart. You'll see grander ones later, though, I assure you.

While living your way into each new emotion, continue to tell new, better feeling, believable stories about your desire from that emotional perspective. Once again, do this just as I teach you in my books and on my website.

You should also continue to let yourself be inspired to create games and activities to keep you focused on your alignment with your desire. Once again, in Chapter Seven, I'll give you examples of games and activities I created and used. Additionally, the Hicks' book *Ask and It Is Given* has a large section devoted to games and activities you might also find helpful.

You will also undoubtedly notice that your perspectives change as you move up the chart. What you might have thought you would be thinking about and writing about often turns out very differently in real practice by the time you get to that emotional perspective. For example, I might have started writing about financial abundance thinking that the way I'd eventually manifest it would be for the universe to motivate people to buy lots of my books. That may have seemed like the most logical way for financial abundance to manifest.

But now, way up the Emotional Reference Chart, I no longer have that perspective at all. Instead I have transitioned, in a very natural, slow, steady progression, into focusing on delivering greater value (and imbuing greater value into the work I've already done). That is because from my new emotional perspective (my new beliefs), I now understand that delivering value, and knowing that what I'm providing to the world has great value, is what financial abundance is all about. In fact, that's what abundance in any form is about.

My new beliefs are: If I'm delivering great value, the universe will reflect that back to me. And I don't have to sweat how that will happen. I once thought/fretted, "How will the universe get all those people to buy all the books I'll need to sell to become financially abundant?" But now I believe that all I need focus on is providing and delivering wonderful value—which is a much less stressful belief.

This process, you'll find, is the living embodiment of the old saying, "Until we agree to suffer, there will be no end to the suffering." I used to think that saying was very negative, until I learned how our quantum field creates our material reality. An updated version of that saying for you could be, "Until we admit and accept where our true emotional perspective is about something we desire, our efforts to manifest that desire will only continue to amount to slapping smiley faces over an empty gas tank."

What I've found is that within the course of a few weeks or months (depending on how low on the Emotional Reference Chart I started), I can move up to the highest spots on the chart in regards to the desire on which I've focused. And once I'm there, I'm flying and I stay there. And my new emotional perspective is very real because I've taken great care to retrain my subconscious brain in a slow, deliberate manner—just as I trained that bunny in Keedysville. So much more real than all the pretending, wishing, hoping, self-convincing, and fake-it-'til-I-make-it that I did before.

It might be disappointing to hear that it may take weeks or months to get there, but I can't say this strongly enough: Do not get in a rush and try to shortcut this process. Remember that your subconscious brain needs to be coaxed toward the new beliefs on the higher end of the Emotional Reference Chart just like coaxing that timid rabbit to my porch. This is how your subconscious brain works. Not only is it concerned with keeping you in safe, familiar territory, but it has also been conditioned toward that safe, familiar territory through years of reinforcement. I go into this in more detail later.

Allow me, as your coach, to address some important points about this process. Let's start with the discomfort of "where you are" regarding your desire during this process—especially when you begin, but also while you're at any of the emotional perspectives lower than where you want to be. Those lower perspectives are very uncomfortable, and it's natural to feel discomfort during this process. Why? Any time there is a gap between your emotional perspective (your beliefs) and your desire, there will be discomfort and pain. That is why you don't use this process on things about which you feel no discomfort.

If your perspective on your desire is uncomfortable, it follows that there **must** be a gap between your emotional perspective (your beliefs) and your desire. If there is a painful gap between your beliefs and your desires, the only way to remedy that is to move your beliefs higher to align with your desires. The only other alternative is to actively try to sublimate your desires, to pretend you don't really have them and hope they go away. This is a fool's game because your desires will never abate. They're not supposed to, because you were born to expand and grow into your grandest visions for yourself.

You were born to desire. And there is absolutely nothing wrong with desiring more for yourself. In fact, desiring more is so natural for us, trying to sublimate or deny our desires is one of the most painful things we can do.

I recommend fully embracing your desires. They are God given. Let "People gotta desire" become one of your new stories when you catch yourself chastising yourself for having them. After all, the act of beating yourself up (calling yourself "greedy" for desiring more money, for example) is just a way you've learned to avoid the pain of not achieving those desires.

As an aside, here's a good litmus test for deciding whether your desire is something you should put your energy toward achieving:

1.  Sometimes we desire something so we can **become** happy. This is such an easy trap to fall into. If we're not currently happy, it's quite natural to imagine that attaining something we desire will *make* us happy.

2. The alternative is to already **be** happy and still desire. Wanting what you have (finding ways to truly be appreciative and grateful) while, at the same time, embracing your desires for more—not because fulfilling those desires will *make* you happy, but because you already *are* happy and fulfilling those desires is simply fun and exciting.

Guess which one of those perspectives will bear the most fruit? And which one will produce the results you want? I've put effort into attaining my desires from both perspectives. I can assure you that perspective number one, wanting to fulfill a desire to make you happy, will not only not succeed in the long run, but it can also actually bring a lot of pain into your life.

And if you don't get honest about where you really are, you cannot move up the emotional chart. You cannot move up to better feelings if you continue to pretend you feel better and have better beliefs about your absent desires.

No matter what discomfort you feel from any perspective during this process, weren't you already uncomfortable every day anyway (at least on a subconscious level)? And, unless you keep moving forward and change your beliefs in a substantive, lasting way, won't you always feel uncomfortable? Won't you always be suffering the pain of an absence of that thing you desire greatly?

Once again, the old saying "Until we agree to suffer, there will be no end to the suffering" comes into play.

Being honest about your painfully out-of-alignment beliefs about a long-held desire can sound like you'll be paddling upstream. But remember: You will only be using this process on topics about which you've been feeling pain, feeling discomfort, and/or not manifesting like you want for quite a while. So, every time you use this process, there is obviously already a gap between your belief and your desire.

You've been conditioned by society to dampen your desires as a way to ease the pain of that gap. That doesn't work. That's playing small. The only thing that really works to ease this kind of pain is to raise your beliefs to the level of your desires. And this process allows you to actually retrain your brain and raise your beliefs instead of slapping band-aids on them.

Next let's address feeling snippets of higher emotions while you're writing/living your way into perspectives lower than those snippets. When you are writing from the perspective of lower emotions, you will often feel flashes of hope and other better feelings. That is natural because you not only greatly wish to manifest your desire, but you've also probably been in the habit of periodically giving yourself positive affirmations and thinking positive thoughts about it.

Once again, bear in mind that you are only using this process on a topic that has been causing you discomfort, pain, and where you have been experiencing absence in your life. Obviously, your real, most constant and steady beliefs on this topic are not those better feeling emotional snippets (even though you may be fully able to access the better feeling thought at any time) or you wouldn't be needing to use this process on this topic in the first place.

Don't discount the better feeling thoughts; its fine to feel good about your desire, even if only briefly. Just make sure you re-focus on the current emotional perspective you're writing about and living your way into, which is lower than the snippet of higher feelings you might be enjoying.

Focusing on the current emotional perspective you've been writing about doesn't mean you must go around all day dwelling on Worry (or whatever the not-so-good-feeling emotional perspective is) either. Be cognizant of the perspective of Worry and frame your absent desire in those terms while living your way into that perspective, but don't make Worry your dominant focus for everything you experience during those days. But if Worry is truly where you are on the desire for which you're using this process (and if you're feeling discomfort then there **must** be a gap between your beliefs and your desire, right?) then you were already carrying Worry around with you all day anyway. So keep your stories about that desire focused on Worry while you're on that perspective.

Third, let's address feeling snippets of *lower* emotional perspectives during your writing/living your way into higher ones. I call that "backsliding" and, yes, I backslide too. Sometimes backsliding comes from having a case of the HALTS (getting too Hungry, Angry, Lonely, Tired, or Serious). If that's the case, you should quit paying any attention to your lower, less positive perspectives and take care of yourself. Get something to eat, blow off some steam, talk with a friend, get some rest, or find a moment to laugh gently with yourself.

Sometimes you'll simply be resisting the improvement of the new emotional perspective, or belief. When that happens, step back and say, "Gee. I'm resisting. How curious. I wonder why I'm doing that. It's okay for me to do, but where is it coming from and why? After all, this new perspective is only slightly more positive than the previous one; there really is no reason for me to be scared of it." Telling yourself that story immediately puts you back into an allowing and accepting mode. And then, guess what happens? You're no longer resisting.

You should also remember that those old emotional perspectives, which you previously wrote about and lived your way into, are very familiar to you. Remember that old beliefs, even painful or harmful ones, are like your favorite pair of jeans—natural and easy to slip into. Those old neural pathways, after all, don't atrophy and disappear overnight. They do become much less powerful as you form new ones and, thus, use the old pathways less and less. But they stick around awhile, so don't feel disappointed or surprised when you find yourself using them. When that happens, gently redirect your brain by saying, "That's an old belief and I understand why you went there—it's a familiar pathway. But we have authentically moved ourselves up the emotional perspective chart and have new beliefs now. Although I understand why you'd want to think that way, I want to focus on my new beliefs - which we have already embraced and accepted."

I have also found that sometimes when those less positive emotional perspectives creep in, I might have moved up to the next highest emotion too fast. That's called, of course, "slapping a smiley face on it." When I slap on smiley faces, things almost always get at least a little bit scary. The new emotional perspective, or belief, can feel fake. I can feel out of control or even sense impending doom ahead. In that case, I slow down, backtrack, and spend a little more time with the previous emotional perspective I've just moved on from.

When I relax, get into allowing mode, and put my attention and focus back on the previous emotional perspective (or belief) the scary, fake, out-of-control, and impending-doom feelings disappear almost immediately and I'm back on track.

I've found that I start feeling better the moment I move just one tick up the Emotional Reference Chart. For example, Frustration does feel better than Worry. Regarding my desire, is Frustration where I want to be in the long run? Heck no. But I notice immediate relief from just one tick up the chart.

And I also notice that I start to see exciting new manifestations as I move up the chart. With each movement in a better feeling direction, even moving just one emotion up, I begin to manifest and allow manifestations that are a little more aligned with my desires. In this manner, using this process feels a bit like slowly opening the top of a treasure chest. For example, of course Worry/Nervousness doesn't allow as much of my desire to manifest as Joy/Elation will, but Worry/Nervousness does manifest a material reality more aligned with my desire than Anxiety/Fear did, because it is a slightly more positive belief than Anxiety/Fear and, thus, creates slightly more positive expectations, which are then conveyed, unconsciously, to the quantum field.

Based on my experience, your manifestations will start to feel like a steady, powerful flow, strongly aligned with your desires, somewhere around Hopefulness/Optimism. And you won't just experience manifestations more aligned with your desires; you'll see and feel new, improved inspiration and opportunities. So, depending on where you start on the Emotional Reference Chart, a steady flow of aligned manifestations may be only weeks away. Just keep being honest and keep writing; the universe takes care of everything else for you.

This is a good time to address another topic as your coach: a sometimes natural *avoidance* of getting to the highest emotional reference points on the chart. Now you might say, "Is Greg crazy to say this? He must be; I can't *wait* to get up there!" But, believe it or not, I've worked with many people who do avoid writing and living their way up to the highest emotions. They get stuck somewhere amid the first, generally positive, reference points and stop the process.

In my experience, the reasons some people stop their use of this process before reaching the highest emotional reference points are all derived from fear: fear that they are not worthy of greater manifestations—in which case I have often suggested that they stop using this process on the specific desire they had chosen and use it instead to manifest self-worth. Sometimes, fear of what will happen when they get to the highest emotional point on the reference chart is a primal fear about the base unfamiliarity of those higher emotions. Also, there's sometimes a fear that getting to the top of the chart will, in some way, signal that they're "done," and then they unconsciously worry about what they will do next.

We can call those reasons for getting stuck a fear of success. We've all heard that term before, but I've found you can completely discard such fear for at least two reasons:

First, when you allow your desires to manifest, even at the highest levels, you always receive a perhaps unexpected gift in addition to the desire itself: greater desires. Achieving or attaining a milestone only opens us up to still greater desire. And, of course, the good news is that all you need do is continue to raise your beliefs to align with your new, greater, grander desires. The universe isn't a tease—no matter how much you align your beliefs with your current desires, you will always experience the awakening of still greater desires from their manifestation. And you will always have the tools in hand to continue to grow and align with your new, greater desires, because all you'll need to do is continue to use this process to align your beliefs with them.

Second, each day you awaken, you are given the gift of engaging in the most beautiful and exciting game imaginable. It's called "Grow a Greater You." This game is available to you today and, in fact, you're beginning to play it with a lot of power and influence by engaging yourself in this process. And it will always be available to you—even when (or, more accurately, precisely when) your beliefs are at the top of the chart. Moving yourself to the top of the Emotional Reference Chart doesn't end that game. In fact, in many ways it is just the beginning.

Here's a story that illustrates what happens and how this might work for you when you get to the top of the Emotional Reference Chart.

My wife and I recently took a 12-day vacation trip to the Languedoc-Roussillon region of France. Our trip was centered around a watercolor portrait-painting workshop conducted by an amazingly talented artist (and a wonderful person), Ted Nuttall. My wife is the painter; she paints abstractly in oils (but has worked primarily as a sculptor).

My wife hadn't painted professionally with watercolor and she hadn't ever painted a portrait professionally. But because she is an artist, she went to this watercolor portrait workshop with beliefs already somewhere around Interest/Inquisitiveness on the Emotional Reference Chart because of her successful experience as an artist and her natural interest in the new medium.

The workshop lit a fire in my wife, and her work elicited exuberant praise from Ted. She painted a portrait of one of our sons and did a beautiful job. She did such great work and had so much fun, in fact, that, toward the end of the workshop, she moved herself up to the level of Joy/Elation on the Emotional Reference Chart. During our nightly discussions about the workshop, it was obvious to me that my wife was actually not far from Love/Ecstasy as we talked about making changes to her workshop at home to accommodate more work in watercolor.

So, while she didn't intentionally work this process on "painting watercolor portraits", it's appropriate to say that my wife moved herself to very high emotions (and beliefs) around watercolor and portraits. She manifested her goal or desires regarding those two areas.

But is my wife "finished" with "watercolor" and "portraits"? Of course not. Even though she is now at the highest levels of the Emotional Reference Chart concerning those two desires, she has merely begun a new journey called "Grow a Greater Watercolor Portrait Painter." This game is the same one she began to play at the beginning of the workshop, only now she is playing it from an even higher emotional reference point. And now she gets to spend the rest of her life playing that game, if she chooses, from those higher-level beliefs.

As I'm sure you can surmise, a painter only gets better and refines her techniques the more she paints. Thus, the more time she spends playing this game, the grander her desires for "Growing a Greater Watercolor Portrait Painter" will become as her talent grows. And as her desires continue to grow with each "level" of growth she attains as a watercolor portrait painter, she merely needs to continue to raise her beliefs to align with her new, grander desires.

It works the same way for any of us, in any area of our lives.

For example, when I first used this process on financial abundance, I had my tail between my legs. I had thought I knew all about how to use the law of attraction to manifest wealth, so I started a real estate business in the late 1990s. I had taken a lot of great action, and focused on nothing but positive thoughts and feelings but, in the end, I had ultimately been trying to "create" wealth instead of raising my beliefs by moving up the Emotional

Reference Chart and allowing my beliefs to align with my desire for more wealth. Because I didn't yet understand that changing my beliefs about money was the most important thing for me to do, six years later I was $1,000,000 in debt, facing scads of foreclosures, and saw certain bankruptcy on the horizon—not to mention scaring, disappointing, and angering my family.

In my desperate state, I eventually learned how to move myself up the Emotional Reference Chart. Consequently, I was able to craft the process I'm now teaching you.

Using the same process you have just learned and are beginning today, I got rid of that debt. I never had to declare bankruptcy, I never had any foreclosures, and I now have more money in my life than I ever even dared dream of back during those dark days (when I would have cut off one of my arms simply to have my head above water).

Does that mean I am "done" with financial abundance? Heck no. As I've continued to manifest my desires regarding financial abundance, I've always found that still greater desires awaken. And they can all be allowed to manifest by continuing to play this amazing game called "Grow a Greater Greg." Even though I am world's wealthier than I dared desire back in 2006, I am still actively raising my beliefs around financial abundance. I continue to see a new physical reality as I continue to raise my beliefs. I continue to receive new inspirations for joyous action and expansion from the quantum field as I continue to raise my beliefs. And I continue to see new opportunities manifest right in front of my eyes as I continue to raise my beliefs.

The same is true for my desires about my body, my health, my family, my relationships, my self-worth, my career, etc. In all those areas, I am allowing greater desires to manifest than I ever would have dared dream prior to crafting this process and learning how to raise my beliefs to align with them. In fact, today, I often don't even create specific dreams; I definitely have desires for even grander expansion in all those areas and plans in place to attain them, but I no longer put handcuffs on the universe by setting limits of any kind on my expansion.

Today, I dare to expand into the limitless creativity and abundance of the quantum field. There is truly no end to this game, and I'm so glad that you, too, have decided to join me and thousands of others who dare to expand in this wonderful manner. Through this process, you now have the opportunity to expand into your greatest version (and vision) of yourself and put an end to your cycle of suffering.

# Chapter Six—Additional Coaching From Questions Asked Most Frequently While Using My Process

This chapter is crafted from some of the best, most useful tips and insights I've shared with my coaching clients while they worked this process. It is also written to answer the most frequently asked questions I get from people just like you while they are using the process you've just learned. You might think of this chapter as a conversation you're having with your law of attraction coach. If I were sitting down with you to coach you once a week, you'd hear me repeating the information in this chapter frequently—to remind you and keep you on track. So you may want to return to this chapter periodically for just such reminders.

This chapter, as well as the previous one and the next two, will address your most common questions and concerns while working this process. Your experiences may not be identical to mine (and others who've worked this process to retrain their brain) and that's okay. It's not important, perhaps, that you have a mirror image of my experiences; what is important is that you work this process diligently—exactly as I've written. As long as you apply yourself to it, your brain will develop new neural pathways, which will become your new beliefs and send new expectations to the quantum field. And, through those new expectations, your material reality will align itself more and more readily with your desires.

## When Shouldn't I Use this Process?

As you've read, this process I use and have taught you replaces the old, ineffective technique of "slapping a smiley face" on the pain of your absent desires. It replaces the "if I never look in that closet, the mess doesn't really exist" paradigm. I want to remind you that I've never encountered any bad feelings, using this process, that I'm not already dealing with everyday anyway—no matter how stuffed down, denied, and glossed over those feelings might have been.

At the risk of repeating myself, let me clarify: You're only using this process on issues that are causing you pain and on desires where you are having obvious, long-term difficulty manifesting. You don't use this process when you are merely having a bad day, feeling low energy, or feeling down. Certainly, for situations like those, it would usually be silly to work your way up the Emotional Reference Chart one emotion at a time.

No, the topics you use these techniques on are ones where a large gap exists between your beliefs and your desires. And for such topics I've found it very helpful to advance slowly and thoughtfully. Why? Because you've usually invested a great deal of time and energy slapping band-aids on the topic in an effort to cover up the bad feelings you've had because of their absence and to make yourself feel better—without ever really looking at it honestly.

If you had been looking at it as honestly and thoroughly as this process requires, you undoubtedly wouldn't be feeling the big gap, the pain of the distance between your low beliefs and your high desires.

For less serious issues/topics where you have mostly been experiencing the manifestation of your desires, you should often be able to jump right up to Joy or Love with a healthy pivoting of your perspective. Reading an inspiring book, getting feedback from an enlightened, positive friend, or listening to a great, high-vibration song can be enough to pivot you out of your temporary pothole. You don't need to take the time to stop at each emotional reference point for those types of temporarily low times.

So when you are experiencing a rogue blip of resistance, it is not necessary to do this inside work. You can just pivot yourself back into a place of allowing your better feeling emotional perspective (or beliefs) about your desire.

I want to reiterate that just one move up the Emotional Reference Chart for a long-term bugaboo (like money, self worth, relationships, etc.) brings relief and new manifestations appearing out of the quantum field. You may not even be that high up the chart yet, but you're higher up the chart than you were 12 days ago. And you'll be noticing some cool stuff manifesting out of the quantum field because of your new, improved, unconscious expectations that have arisen from your new, improved beliefs.

### How Do Beliefs (and Expectations) Actually Send Commands to the Quantum Field?

The analogy I'm about to give is verified by quantum physics.

You are like a piano in terms of how you interact with the quantum field. When you strike a key on a piano, it causes a hammer to fall on a chord and a specific note is created. The note is created by the vibration of the chord you have struck by hitting the key.

Your beliefs, and the expectations that unconsciously arise from them, are the keys on your personal piano. You are creating notes every second of every day through the vibrations of your beliefs and their attending expectations. And, in our universe, like vibrations attract one other.

Energy, you see, forms material objects when it becomes coherent, or in-synch, with you. So your vibrations, your beliefs and the expectations that naturally and unconsciously arise from them, are the medium of communication between you and the quantum field.

I like to think of my bad-feeling, out-of-alignment beliefs and expectations as the deep, bass keys on my piano and the good-feeling, in-alignment beliefs and expectations as the higher keys on my piano. And my every belief (and attending expectation) strikes a chord, sending a vibration out into the universe, commanding the quantum field to create my material experiences.

The practice of moving up the Emotional Reference Chart one emotion at a time is just like moving up the scale on a piano keyboard one key at a time. Before too long, you're playing only the good-feeling, aligned-with-your-desires notes on your piano.

## What Else Can I Do Besides Tell Better-Feeling Stories and Moving Myself Up the Emotional Reference Chart?

Are you meditating? If not, I can't recommend it highly enough, especially while you're working this process. Meditation can put you in direct contact with the quantum field because the limitless potential of that field is accessible in the space between your thoughts. That space is where boundless creativity and abundance exist. That space is where all your material manifestations come from. Being in contact with the quantum field, therefore, is not only calming and reassuring, it's incredibly motivating.

I'm no expert on meditation, but here's what works for me:

### Sitting/Resting Meditation

I learned this technique from Wayne Dyer, and it works very well. Sit cross-legged and touch your thumb to your middle finger on each hand. Picture a large movie screen with the words "Our" and "Father" on the screen bigger than life. Then focus on the blank space between "Our" and "Father."

All the while chant "Ahhhhhh" (according to some, the "name" of the universal mind or, if you will, God) and imagine good feelings flowing up from your groin to your head. Feelings like love, freedom, and abundance. Try to do this for at least fifteen minutes at a time.

When ordinary thoughts arise, do your best to let them float away. You might imagine a gentle breeze continually blows and carries any intrusive thoughts you have away on it.

On most days, while you meditate like this you will be able to spend a few moments without any problem thoughts—without any thoughts at all, for that matter. Thus, you will be in a state of no resistance. It not only feels wonderful, but it's also a powerful way to allow your new beliefs to interact with the quantum field in an unadulterated manner.

## Waking Meditation

At any point in your day, you can enter a state of having no thoughts at all. Of making no internal judgments about anything that's happening. To do this, simply practice letting that breeze blow your thoughts out of your head, just as you do during your sitting/resting meditation. When you have no thoughts, you are accessing the quantum field, so this is a form of active, waking meditation. And this technique is available to you any time at all because you can still concentrate on your task at hand while doing this.

Additionally, during the day, whenever you feel resistance (or lower, bad-feeling emotions and beliefs), mentally step back and say, "Oh, I'm resisting. How curious; that is interesting. What am I resisting? I don't have to do that." That acceptance of your resistance (rather than trying to fight it) usually releases it, and you can jump right back into the stream of your current, better-feeling emotional focus and beliefs.

Isn't it satisfying to see your perception of the value of what you do and who you are rise as you progress up the Emotional Reference Chart? And, in turn, to have the quantum field reflect that value back to you by sending love and appreciation back to you in myriad forms?

### *I'm Having Difficulty Letting Go of My Old "I'll Believe It When I See It" Paradigm - What Can I Do to Help Move Past That?*

Here are two things I've learned as I've retrained my brain about any beliefs I've held concerning desires I've greatly wished to manifest:

First, have you ever gone for a jog and been dripping with sweat when you finish? Your jog over, you lean forward and grab your shorts to stretch and rest, and your sweat drips off your forehead and hits the pavement.

You weren't sweating so profusely because you leaned forward and grabbed your shorts, were you? No, of course not. Your sweat was coming from the hearty exercise you were engaged in twenty minutes earlier. The sweat you were experiencing represented the results of your previous exercise, not the stretching you were doing at that moment.

Your present material reality works the same way. Whatever and whoever currently surrounds you is the culmination of your past beliefs and actions, not your current ones. Looking at your present reality as anything else is folly.

So do not make the mistake of defining yourself by what you see and experience when you look at your current circumstances. Your current circumstances often have little to do with your new beliefs and how you are commanding the quantum field to form your material reality through your new expectations today. And in the future, you will manifest different things that are more aligned with your desires because of today's new, better-feeling beliefs and expectations.

That's great news if you find yourself in an undesirable situation (like I did so many years ago) such as an unfulfilling relationship, an empty bank account, or a mountain of debt. Free yourself from the self-made prison of defining yourself by your present circumstances and surroundings.

Second, remember that everyone and everything else in the world is really only you in a different package. And, in turn, you are the same thing as everyone and everything else in the world—just in your own unique package. So if you desire more customers for your business, all you're seeking is for you to give yourself money. If you desire to be happy, all you're seeking is to see your own most exalted beauty and self-worth reflected back to you in your life experiences. Or if you desire a soul mate, all you're seeking is for you to meet the highest version of yourself.

What the heck am I talking about?

The material world is formed from a big ocean of (mostly) hydrogen, oxygen, carbon, and nitrogen. That ocean is the quantum field. From this ocean, every single material person, place, or thing is manifested. No matter how different two things may be, they were both once just part of this big quantum ocean in which we live and from which all things are formed. Everything is made from the same stuff and comes from the same source. Every single thing in the material world is just some unique combination of mostly hydrogen, oxygen, carbon, and nitrogen.

Think of a warm spot in the Pacific Ocean. That warm spot remains even though billions of water molecules are passing through it each second, temporarily becoming part of the warm spot and then quickly leaving it to become a different part of the Pacific. You are like a warm spot in the ocean.

I've heard it said that the ocean is the universal mind (or God) and you are a wave on that ocean. And just as a wave is what the ocean is doing, you are what the universal mind is doing.

There are billions and billions of warm spots in this quantum ocean, the quantum field. Each warm spot is a person, or a flower, or a candle, or a clock, or a dollar bill, etc. But all the warm spots are just a part of this quantum ocean—irrespective of how diverse they may be when compared with one another.

That puts a different perspective on desiring new material experiences and manifesting your desires, doesn't it? All you have to do is get yourself in a place where you know you deserve more love and more reflected value from yourself. If you raise your beliefs and simply become those things you desire, you will be and have those things as naturally as rain falls from a pregnant cloud. And you'll soon be manifesting material experiences much more closely aligned to your desires than you may have previously dreamed. Lucky for you, you're working on a process, right now, that will get you to that place and will allow you to become the very things you desire.

## What Role Do My Feelings Play?

Meditating and turning off your brain are ways to commune with the quantum field, or the universal mind. Yet you already have a ready-made channel of information from the quantum field—your emotions. Emotions are your primary, direct feedback regarding how aligned (or unaligned) your beliefs are with your desires. Your emotions tell you what your beliefs are—that's why raising them retrains your subconscious brain to have new beliefs. Just as a thermometer tells you you're sick by showing that your body temperature is too high, feeling bad about something you desire signals to you that your beliefs are not in alignment with that thing. And vice-versa: Feeling better about something you desire (as you're doing while you retrain your brain through this process) signals to you that you are more in alignment with it.

You have the quantum field, the universal mind, around you every moment of every day. And through your emotions and meditation (both seated and walking) you are connected to it and communicating with it. Increasing and enabling that connection only allows a more full realization of your desires.

It is scientifically true that there are as many universes are there are observers. That is why the process of moving up the emotional chart works so well: You see a different universe when you feel, or vibrate, differently about your desires.

You live in a different universe than me. We could go see the movie *World War Z* together, sit beside each other, and watch the same exact film, yet experience two completely different movies (i.e., you love it/I hate it). I know that's almost a trite example, but it does correctly illustrate this principle.

## *What Can I Expect From These New Perspectives?*

By the way, you may be surprised by what comes out while you are writing about and living your way into each new, slightly more positive emotional perspective on your desire. Sometimes you will find that, where you imagined an emotional perspective to be almost wholly negative, it contains some rather positive nuances. Sometimes you'll find rather unexpected insights that help you experience a more positive perspective, even from the emotions that you might figure to be only negative. The main reason for this is that each new emotional perspective is slightly more positive and slightly more empowering than the previous one.

Sometimes you might think, "Why should I write about my desire from (this particular emotional perspective)? It doesn't make any sense." I've taught you that the way you move into a new feeling perspective, the way you retrain your brain about an absent desire, is to write, freeform, how that issue will look/feel/sound/taste/smell/etc. from that new perspective. For example, what will financial freedom feel like from the perspective of Pensiveness/Melancholy? Often, it's while writing for one of the emotional perspective that don't seem to make sense that a big smack upside the head comes—an unexpected insight that totally rocks your world and changes your viewpoint forever. Give each emotion its own day. Try it, play with it. You'll be amazed.

Even with the negative emotional perspectives, you'll find there are almost always tinges of hope and other good emotions. But if positive emotions are your dominant feelings about a desire you hold, you don't need to use this process on it. You don't need to *become* it; you're already there!

In other words, if you feel good about something already, you're not going to be writing about it and using this process on it in the first place.

### *This Doesn't Feel Like the Way I've Learned to Do Things in the Past - Why Does it Feel So Different?*

This very topic is something I discussed recently with a man who took this process to Las Vegas. With limited poker experience, he sat down at some pro-level poker tables and came away with more money than he started. He used this process to rocket through (but not cheat) the normal learning curve for playing poker.

And that's what you're doing here, too. You're learning to retrain your subconscious brain to enhance, and even rocket through, the normal learning process. You're still engaging the normal learning process and training your subconscious brain the way it is always trained, but you're just doing it more quickly than normal. And, of course, you're doing it intentionally and building new beliefs (new neural pathways) of your choosing, which serve you and facilitate the manifestation of your desires.

Think about it. How do you learn something? How do you "know" you can do something or be something?

You practice and practice and practice, under the guidance of a teacher or coach, until you know you are what you desire. Achieving a promotion, earning a degree, having a successful marriage, lifting weights, becoming an accountant, running a marathon, being an elite poker player, driving a race car, etc., are usually all accomplished in this manner.

Quantum physics tell us the equation for manifesting a desire: First you learn it, then you practice it, then you believe it, then you see it, because, in the end, when you are successfully manifesting it, you <u>are</u> it.

By retraining your brain in this manner you are simply starting a normal learning process (which almost always leads to the eventual achievement of a desired outcome) at the "then you believe it" portion of this equation. And you are doing this by retraining your brain through intentionally raising your emotional perspectives (your beliefs) about your desire.

This is a magical process and it really does work (as you are undoubtedly already discovering). It is not "cheating" (although other people might not think it's fair that you skipped all the blood, sweat, and tears they may have gone through to achieve a similar desire). It is simply taking advantage of the leading-edge knowledge and awareness you now possess.

### How Can I Stop Focusing on the Absence of My Desire When the Plain Fact Is: I Don't Have It?

This also leads us into a very similar topic. You don't want or need the things you have because you already have them. In other words, when you focus on wanting or needing something, you will never have it; the only way to have something is to know you have it—to be it. So, how in the world can you stop wanting or needing something you don't currently have, when the plain, simple fact is that you don't have it yet?

Simple: Focus on being it. This works excellently with the process you just learned. Simply imagine the feelings you'll have when your desire manifests in your life. Then, rather than focus on how much you want or need that desire, focus on being that thing you desire by having those feelings it will give you. Right now. For no reason at all other than you've decided to. And any time you catch yourself wanting or needing that thing you desire, remind yourself to, instead, be that thing by feeling the feelings you expect it to give you.

### What's the Difference Between this Process You're Teaching Me and Positive Affirmations/Thoughts?

Finally, a word about positive affirmations. Many people, with the best intentions, use affirmations and positive thinking in lieu of the belief-raising you are doing. You may have tried this too and discovered how ineffective affirmations are for long-term, positive change. This is because people don't understand (yet) how powerfully their beliefs command the quantum field and how challenging it is to change a belief, to retrain their subconscious brain. Used in lieu of the belief-raising process you've learned (or in lieu of a normal "learn, practice, believe, see, be" process), positive affirmations and positive thinking are just smiley faces on an empty tank.

Using positive affirmations and positive thinking adjunctively with this process can be powerful. As long as you don't avoid looking honestly at each emotional perspective on the chart (so you can feel it, live it, be it, and, eventually, move past it), positive affirmations and positive thinking can become additional rocket fuel on your very real journey of retraining your brain and fulfilling your desires.

But I recommend that you focus more upon telling yourself better-feeling, believable stories about your current circumstances (as I teach more extensively in my other books), rather than focus primarily on positive affirmations. Because of what we know about the human brain, changing beliefs is virtually impossible to accomplish through positive affirmations, which is probably one of the main reasons you may have been frustrated by trying to use them in the past.

The main trouble with using positive thoughts or affirmations alone, as you know, is that your subconscious mind does not really believe them. Your conscious mind hears them and you feel good in that moment. But because your subconscious mind knows that those positive thoughts or affirmations don't reflect your true underlying beliefs, they are like putting a bandage on a broken arm.

Luckily, you have learned how to retrain your subconscious brain properly, reforming your beliefs to naturally create expectations aligned with your desires. All the reformation process requires is some patience and a commitment to the process revealed in the beginning of this book. Your patience is required because creating new beliefs (and, thus, new expectations) is not an overnight process. But rest assured—your patience will be rewarded. Although you probably won't realize your ultimate desires tomorrow, you will begin to experience positive changes almost immediately upon entering into this process.

# Chapter Seven—The Story of My Personal Experience with Using My Process for the First Time

Now let's get into my personal experience using this process. Although my results may sound magical, even challenging to believe, everything you read really happened for me. It didn't happen because I was lucky; it happened as a direct result of using the process I'm teaching you in this book. And I've found that it only gets easier to perform this process with practice. Since my initial foray, I've used it to manifest my desires concerning my health, weight, family, relationships, self-worth, marriage, etc.

What I did (and continue to do) with this process is not an anomaly. You can do it too. In fact, I encourage you not to limit yourself to merely duplicating my success; there is no reason you can't do even better.

In June of 2007, I got a phone call from my attorney telling me that she could hold off the banks only until September. After that, foreclosures would ensue and I would be left with no choice but to declare bankruptcy. With a failed rental property business of fifteen rental homes in various stages of unrentable (and, with my means at the time, largely irrepairable) condition, I was a little over $1,000,000 in debt and had no means to repay any of it. And the dilapidated states of these homes meant no one in their right mind was willing to buy them for anything close to their mortgage amounts.

In addition to making my life a living hell, my business failures had also driven a wedge between my wife and me. They were not the cause of our problems but they put our difficulties under a microscope and dialed them up to ten. My family was rightfully scared, disappointed, and angry with me. I put them under incredible stress after I had all but promised them only fantastic returns from my endeavors.

Flash forward to May of 2008. On a Monday afternoon, I got a phone call from my realtor, telling me that the last of my properties was going to be sold and the bank was forgiving all of my remaining debt (just as all but one of the previous ones had). After that phone call, I had finally gotten rid of every single rental property, never had any foreclosures, had no remaining debt, never had to declare bankruptcy, and actually had money in the bank.

How did that happen? And how can you repeat my successes, or, better yet, exceed them?

Quite simply, it happened for me not because I desired it so badly. I did desire it more than anything else in my life, but my desire wasn't the key. It happened for me because I used the process you've just learned to retrain my brain, aligning my beliefs about financial abundance with my desires for it. And you can use the same process to retrain your brain, to align your beliefs with any desire you wish—perhaps on an even grander scale than I have done.

This process took my family from sure bankruptcy to a release from litigation, debt forgiveness, and financial excess in less than a year. As amazing as that might sound, it's not an overhyped version of what happened after I created and employed this process. What actually happened is much more fantastic then you might believe—and all because of this process.

During the time between June 2007 and May 2008, I had large checks arrive unexpectedly in the mail. I had bills "mysteriously" be far less than I expected. I had money appear in my checking account seemingly out of thin air. I had banks tell me they would accept far less than I owed on properties, so I could short sell them, and then tell me I didn't have to repay almost $700,000 in loans. At one point, in fact, my attorney said to me, "Greg, I have no idea why {this bank} is being so good to you!" But I knew why—because that's what my new beliefs about financial abundance were commanding the quantum field to manifest in my material reality.

At one point, in fact, an attorney who was involved with all the various short sales and debt forgiveness just about fell out of his chair, saying, "Why in the hell would they (the banks) do that for you?!" When he said that, I had an initial flash of extreme fear, "Oh no! He's right! The banks won't really do this for me." Then I quickly relaxed, remembering that the universe will move people and mountains to fulfill my desires when my beliefs are aligned with them. I quickly decided to use his reaction as an affirmation of how absolutely powerful and ironclad is the promise that we cannot have a desire that the universe will not fulfill if we've aligned our beliefs with it.

While working this process for the first time on financial abundance, I discovered that we are the ones who dream small and play small—not the quantum field. The universe doesn't know the difference between manifesting a penny on the sidewalk versus manifesting a bank saying, "Greg, we'll let you sell this property for far less than it's worth...you don't need to go bankrupt...and, I tell you what, instead of going bankrupt, why don't you just forget about this huge loan for which we have you liable, lock, stock, and barrel?"

Here is a specific example: At one point, I had finally sold a huge albatross of a property by getting the bank to agree to a short sale. The buyer paid cash and planned to rehab it. There were some snags on my end, which delayed the sale for a couple of weeks. The buyer became increasing agitated, for various reasons, and called my realtor on two occasions demanding reductions in his purchase price. Both times we gave him reductions amounting to a total discount of $3,500.

I never stressed on the loss of money, which, because of my mortgage contract, would be added to the amount I would be short to the bank. I never focused on this potentially being added to the amount of money the bank might end up holding me responsible for. I just said, "Thank you, God. Thank you, Universe, for lining up this buyer. I trust that everything is happening just like it's supposed to. I'm not going to call this bad because I not only lack the perspective to do so, but labeling it so would also tie the hands of the quantum field's infinite potential to allow everything to happen just like it's supposed to."

At the closing, the buyer showed up and paid us the full purchase price. There was no mention of any of the discounts he had demanded and no anger on his part. Believe me, this buyer was an experienced buyer, an old hand at the real estate business. He didn't just forget to give us $3,500 less for the property. He just chose not to. I had no explanation for that other than the explanation I had for every other way my desires were manifesting: My beliefs were aligned with my desires and the quantum field was following suite.

Here's a synopsis of how this process worked for me:

In early summer, 2006, I finally had to admit that my real estate rental business was doomed. For six-plus years, my business had been hemorrhaging money and I had only been able to stay one step ahead by using "tomorrow's money" to keep the mortgages paid. But, over the course of time, I reached a point where, due to lack of cash flow, I was no longer able to keep the properties in good enough shape to re-rent when a vacancy occurred. As this issue snowballed, I began to confront vandalism and property damage that finally completely sunk me. All but a few of the properties became dilapidated.

When I finally put up the white flag, with great fear, I contacted an attorney and began following her advice. I put up all the properties for sale. Not having the money to make mortgage payments, I certainly had no money to hire help for the needed rehab efforts, so I spent my weekends working on my houses to get them in saleable condition. It was a time of tremendous fear and depression for me and incredible fear and stress for my family, because we could all see what was surely coming:

complete financial devastation and the loss of much of what we held dear in our lives.

Unfortunately for me, the bottom dropping out of the housing market coincided with my circumstances. Even if the properties had been in pristine condition, buyers would not have been willing to pay enough for my rental houses to pay off the mortgages I owed on them. Hence, my realtors were giving me nothing but bad news—even though we were listing the homes for only what I owed. It was a perfect storm for foreclosures and bankruptcy. I patched up and cleaned up the homes, but they still were in too poor a condition to command even near-market value, while, at the same time, no one was paying anything close to near-market value for investment properties—let alone residential properties.

For a little over a year I continually worked on my homes while my realtors tried to sell them. I never received anything close to good news during this period regarding a potential sale. During this time, I could see little else but foreclosures looming, bankruptcy on the horizon, and the painful dissolution of my family, as a direct result of the incredible stress produced by this situation. We envisioned losing our home, many of our possessions, and being deep in debt for the rest of our lives.

The banks, of course, were growing increasingly agitated. I owed about $1,000,000 in mortgage debt and had stopped making any payments on the rental properties because all I could afford to do was keep our primary residence current and pay our monthly bills. We were inundated daily with phone calls and letters from the banks who, understandably, wanted their money. Sheriff's deputies showed up at my home and workplace on a regular basis, delivering official notices of litigation and court action from banks. It was a frightening time for all of us.

As the situation continued to worsen, I grew more and more depressed—to the point where the thought of ending my life as a way out sometimes didn't seem like a bad idea. I also grew angrier and angrier with God and the universe. I was a good person. I had had the best of intentions when I started this business, and I really felt that I was being punished for some unknown reason. And it only made matters worse that my family would be punished too—all because of me.

You see, when I started this business in 1998, I had done so within what I thought was the proper applications of any successful endeavor. I had studied the power of positive thought for years and found it to be a powerful tool. My life was rich with success and I honestly thought that this business would be the final step to move my family over the threshold of true financial abundance and freedom. Although, in retrospect, one can easily critique my methods of creating this business (I certainly could have done many things better), I was definitely focused upon positive action in every step I took.

I made sure my immediate family was on board at the start. I made sure I was surrounded with people and information that would shepherd my business and ensure its success. I spent time working on my business on a regular basis, meeting frequently with tenants and my property manager. I journaled each day about my business from a positive perspective. I spoke about the business in only positive terms. I meditated each day on the success of my business. And when I had small setbacks, I always found a way to stay positive about my business. Until the very end, I refused to see my business as a negative endeavor. Because of my commitment to positive thought, I could not imagine this business failing to produce the results I so greatly desired. "After all," I thought, "the universe will surely respond to my positive intent, thought, and action."

In fact, during the year or so that I was trying to sell all my properties, I honestly thought that the universe was going to be stepping in at any moment, like a white knight, and provide solutions to the failing business so that I wouldn't have to experience complete financial ruin. As time passed, during that year, I became more and more depressed, and angrier and angrier with God. I didn't stop working hard, but my faith in the power of positive thought, God, and the universe was destroyed.

I felt sick to my stomach when I looked at my extensive library of books on the power of positive thought and was completely disillusioned about my personal power to influence my life in positive ways.

It just so happened, however, that about a month prior to that fateful phone call from my attorney in June 2007, an old college friend sent me a book called *The Secret*. Although I had been an ardent student of positive thought, for some reason, I had never studied the law of attraction in any depth or detail. In my jaded state, I refused to read *The Secret*; I wanted no part of any more "positive thought garbage." But I did put it on my bookshelf.

After getting that fateful phone call from my attorney and honestly accepting that we had only a few more months before the financial holocaust hit our family, I took *The Secret* off my bookshelf. After all, I had nothing left to lose. All of my hard work and that of my realtors and attorney had produced nothing more than a delay of the inevitable. I owned 15 rental properties in various states of disrepair, had no renters, no money, no buyers for the properties, and no hope.

I read *The Secret*, with a mind slightly open by the incredible pain we were all suffering and had a positive reaction. The law of attraction made sense to me and I caught a glimmer of hope from it. I thought, "What if the law of attraction could provide solutions for me? What in the hell do I have to lose by trying it?" I felt I was about to lose it all regardless.

But I also realized that, if I wanted to employ the law of attraction, I needed to find some instructions for using it. To that end, after some Internet searching, I was introduced to the work of Jerry and Esther Hicks. As a fan of Wayne Dyer, when I discovered that Dr. Dyer endorsed the Hicks, I decided to read their book *Ask and It is Given*.

*Ask and It is Given* was a revelation to me. As a student of quantum physics, I immediately began making connections between what they wrote about the law of attraction and what I already knew about what quantum physics had to say about our power to influence our material reality. I could see, very plainly, how I had gone so wrong with my business endeavors: I had focused completely upon action without ensuring that my beliefs behind the action were congruent with it. This jibed with what I knew about how our universe worked, through my study of quantum physics, and it truly seemed that I had discovered the missing keys from what I had previously thought was my complete working understanding of the power of positive thought.

My failures made sense to me now. And I felt that I now had the missing ingredients at hand to save my family. Combined with my work ethic, I actually felt that I now possessed the solutions to my dilemma. But, I wondered, did I stumble upon this information too late? Foreclosures and bankruptcy were, after all, four to six months away and I had received not so much as a morsel of good news from my realtors or attorney for over a year.

Once again, I thought, what do I have to lose? I was truly in a no-lose position. If I used the law of attraction to resolve this crisis and it failed, I certainly wouldn't be any worse off than I would be if I didn't. And, what if it did work? I had confidence in my character and work ethic, so why wouldn't I try to add the law of attraction to what I was already doing to resolve our crisis?

Having read the Hicks' recommendation that painful, long-absent desires might have a lot to do with deeply held personal beliefs being out of alignment with those desires, I created a method to improve my beliefs. The method I created is, of course, the one you've just learned. So, in June 2007, I began to use this method just as I've instructed you to.

I need to let you know that my sense of complete desperation and the extremely painful circumstances I was dealing with motivated me to focus on using this method each day like it was the most important thing in my life. I love my family and I also love my job—but I made working on this method an even higher priority than those two things. Though I took care to remain a faithful father and husband and a productive employee, this process became my first and highest focus each day.

And my passion for this process, borne from my unbelievable pain and total desperation, allowed me to move relatively quickly up the chart. It usually only took me one day to truly live myself into the next highest emotional perspective, and then I was able to keep moving up the chart relatively quickly. You may not find that this pace works for you because you may not be as desperate as I was. That's not a bad thing. In fact, I've found that it takes me a little longer to move up the chart today because I have nowhere near the pain and desperation I had when I first employed this process.

You already know the steps I took, as they're explained in detail in Chapter Five. I began my writing from the emotional perspective of Depression/Hopelessness regarding financial abundance and went from there. And I focused on the process with all of my energy each and every single day. Of course, my writings from the lower emotional perspectives were mostly full of negative things. Those were my true feelings and beliefs about money at the time.

But by the time I was merely up to the perspective of Grief/Desolation, I could already see and feel the difference and improvement in not only my state of being, but also in my material experiences. At the lower perspectives, even though I knew my beliefs had not yet been raised to where I wanted them to be eventually, I could tell that this process was real and was making a noticeable difference in my life. So, even from the lower emotional perspectives, I began to develop a strong sense of hope in the process I had created (if not yet in my beliefs about money).

I knew, even from the lower emotional perspectives, my beliefs about money would get where I wanted them to, eventually, and I also knew that my material experiences would be much more aligned with my desires when that happened. And, throughout the process, in addition to the positive experiences with my state of being and my material manifestations, I was continually motivated by the thought, "What do I have to lose?"

By early August, I began to have some real, concrete manifestations. By this time, I was writing from the perspective of Anticipation/Eagerness and higher. Bills were lower than expected, for no reason. Money appeared in my bank ledger unexpectedly. Cash and funds manifested out of thin air. And, perhaps most importantly, I was gifted with new insights and inspirations for positive action that I couldn't see, and weren't available to me, from my previous, lower emotional perspectives about financial abundance. Just as quantum physics tells us that each individual sees her own unique universe, I found that, with each movement up the emotional perspective chart, a whole new world became available to me. I saw new opportunities blossoming all around me with each step up the chart, and it was a very exciting time indeed.

I'll discuss some of those inspirations and opportunities that came into my perspective and understanding a little later in this chapter. For now, here are some excerpts from my journal. Some of them may sound a bit unbelievable (they certainly did to some attorneys I was working with), yet you already know what the end results of this process were for me. I'll ask you to excuse my sometimes "over-the-top" use of exclamation points; I was so excited while writing and I intentionally wanted to keep that excitement going:

July 5, 2007: *"I've been writing about my beliefs and using my process diligently. It's been making a huge difference (improvement) in my daily experiences. My beliefs about some things just don't serve me, I'm finding.*

*For example, after writing about it I realized that I believed that 'I need to be punished for my mistakes.' Also that 'I must earn and deserve good things.' Now...there is nothing inherently wrong with those two beliefs—I am free to believe them if I want.*

*But guess what? I don't want to believe them anymore because they act as resistance to the flow of energy from the quantum field and all good things. So I continue to play a game of 'imagine if those things I believe aren't true.'"*

<u>July 12, 2007</u>: *"I got a great reminder this morning, during meditation, to pour rocket fuel into my writing, my own personal journaling.*

*During the past week and a half, it's become very apparent that I've been using my brain as if it were my mind. What a tough habit to break! But an essential habit to break for us intentional manifestors.*

*The action is not important; the belief, or emotional state, which inspires it is! And the labels and particular techniques of anyone's experience can sometimes become an action-oriented focus for me.*

*If it feels good, it will work."*

<u>July 18, 2007</u>: *"I have experienced a lot of contrast this weekend. My wife and youngest son visited from North Carolina. I viewed this weekend as a chance to see how I was manifesting in relation to my desires. I experienced some amazing highs and some deflating lows.*

*Which, actually, is just about right. Concerning my writing, I'm currently at the emotional reference point of Introspection/Contemplation. I perceive Introspection/Contemplation as a place of in-between energy. Not great/not terrible. Not quite yet ready to quit playing small, but also not quite ready to start playing big. Lots of courage mixed with ample fear.*

*And that's pretty much what got reflected back to me. I'm going to keep writing, because Introspection/Contemplation is not where I want to stay long-term. But I'm also making sure I live myself fully into each emotional perspective. Carefully! No slapping smiley faces over empty gas gauges."*

<u>July 30, 2007</u>: *"Regarding money—I must report that I still rock!!! I rock. I rock. I rock. Thank you universe! 'Cause I love money and money loves me!*

*Imagination is so wonderful and so powerful—our thoughts are real! Over time I can feel my new beliefs taking shape and the old beliefs atrophying."*

August 4, 2007: *"I just checked my account online and found a $1,970 deposit that was made to me today for no reason. I didn't 'work' for it. I didn't 'ask' anyone for it. I just allowed it.*

*And in approximately ten days, we'll receive another $26,000 and we'll get rid of a headache surrounding a property in the process."*

August 9, 2007: *"No way was I doing anything spiritual when I incurred this debt! But I thought I was. I had the best of intentions—but I was all action and no feeling. My beliefs were way south of my actions!*

*If I'm willing to extend value to the universe I can expect the universe to flow it back to me!*

*But, really, that statement is another point to ponder. We each have a 'God in embryo' in us. Waiting to be ushered forth each day. Waiting in the gap between our thoughts."*

August 16, 2007: *"I rock. The Universe rocks. I have such passion for this!!!! It is so awesome to experience the debts melting away!!!!! And the money rolling in from everywhere and anywhere to make it happen."*

August 24, 2007: *"I want to keep this energy river flowing! I'm getting close to wrapping up some more debt and I want to post an update of my money manifestation process.*

*Allowing these manifestations has taken a lot of energy and focus. In the process, I've learned to meditate much more deeply and more effectively! Actually, regarding what I've learned, there is too much to write here! I need to write a book!*

*Thank you universe, of which I am a part!!! Thank you universe, of which I am a worthy co-creator!!! I have so much love, money, joy, companionship, friendship, efficacy, and purpose!!! I have more than enough to fill my heart's desires."*

August 29, 2007: *"The money came yesterday, in the form of forgiven debt. Literally, we owed a bank a loan and the bank said, 'You don't have to pay it back. We'll write it off and you owe us nothing.'*

*Back to self-worth for a moment—self-love is not about finding love flowing to us. It's about finding a way to let love flow through us from the quantum field. When love from the quantum field is flowing through us (to other people, places, and things) then we really experience what we really are. Love. And that is self-love.*

*Just want to check in and say, 'Thank you, Universe!'"*

September 3, 2007: *"Perhaps others have used the process I'm using; it really is very simple. I can't wait to use this process in other areas of my life...other specific topics. It has worked so unbelievably well with the specific topic of 'financial abundance' that I will really enjoy seeing what it will do in these other areas."*

September 17, 2007: *"Since August, I have now paid off $21,575 in debt (using cold hard cash that I simply allowed to manifest)! And, since August, I have allowed banks to forgive $540,272 of debt. (Two attorneys have told me how unbelievable this is...but nothing is unbelievable unless I choose it to be so. And I ain't choosing to 'unbelieve'!!!!)"*

September 23, 2007: *"How well has this process worked? Within the last two-and-a-half-month period I've manifested (or allowed) almost $150,000!!!!*

*Just today it was confirmed: My request was approved and I manifested $40,000 or so for me and my family. And I will soon manifest an additional $150,000 or so in the same manner. I am a money magnet."*

September 28, 2007: *"Today I sent the final payment to close out a $10,000 debt! And I only just started paying on it in October! When I crafted the note accompanying the last check today I wrote, 'I hope this money blesses you—enriches your life. Thank you for giving me the opportunity to share it with you.'"*

October 2, 2007: *"To date, I have gotten banks to forgive over $700,000. As in, 'You don't owe us a dime, Greg.' I've had two attorneys in the last couple months look at me with their mouths agape, saying, 'How in the hell did you get them to agree to that? Why would they do that for you?'"*

October 14, 2007: *"Where I am on this topic: I've taken a couple weeks to meditate on Love/Ecstasy regarding financial abundance. The move from Joy/Elation to Love/Ecstasy is not one I am taking lightly.*

*Feels like I will write about it today, as a matter of fact. Because the egg is hatching, so to speak. My perspective has grown and I'm in a new place of energy and belief."*

October 25, 2007: *"There are as many different universes as there are observers—applying my process is showing me that very clearly. I am utterly amazed at the different perspectives, energies, manifestations, and inspirations which occur at each level of emotion and belief!*

*No wonder some people are happy and successful no matter what's 'occurring' around them...those negatives 'occurrences' aren't actually occurring around 'those people' - just around me! 'Those people' didn't even see or experience the negative because their beliefs are too high up the chart. Except now I'm one of those people too! One of 'those people' who thrive regardless of the circumstances."*

November 19, 2007: *"November has followed suit as a month of tremendous allowing for money manifestation. I'm still waiting to hear final word on our last two pieces of big debt, but my desire is for the banks to forgive those two as they've done the rest.*

*I've paid off almost $30,000 in debt this month! So far! And had another $10,000-plus of debt forgiven. Where does the money come from? You know the answer...I am allowing the universe to share it with me."*

November 27, 2007: *"This morning I was balancing out November's register and updating my debt repayment schedule.*

*I set a goal, back in September, to have a particular debt ($11,000) paid off by the end of 2007. As I updated my records, I saw that with a December payment of $1,900 I will have it paid off! As I updated my checking accounts, I looked for the $1,900 and opened myself up to finding it (as I have done so many times since I started these processes last June).*

*I knew it would be there, yet I only found $900.*

*But that didn't bother me at all! I knew finding the additional $1,000 during the month would be child's play. After all, I've 'found' over $60,000 in cold, hard cash since August. What trouble will the universe have coming up with the additional $1,000 I need to reach my goal of paying off this debt?*

*About 2:30, I got the mail. In the mail I found a check for $1,000! I just sat down and laughed, filled with satisfaction and gratitude.*

*Thank you universe! Can I get an 'Amen'?"*

December 28, 2007: *"I filled out my ledger for December yesterday. I am accustomed to earning approximately $430/month from my website. (I'm referring to the website I have for my Father's business, not anything I've built for LOA teachings). In December, I earned a little over $2,000. All with my mind."*

How did all that happen? There are many things I did every day—things that the Hicks and quantum physics taught me and inspired me to do. But there is one specific thing I did regarding money that poured rocket fuel into my manifestation of it: I decided to celebrate any money, no matter how small the amount, to the maximum extent possible. The inspiration to do this came in early July 2007, when I clearly remembered an instance of receiving money during the darkest days of our financial and personal turmoil.

Here's what I'm referring to: In August, 2006, I opened my mailbox to discover a royalty check from some of my writing. Being $1,000,000 in debt, with no recourse in sight, I was eager to open the envelope. I rushed into my kitchen and opened the envelope to discover a check for $101.07. Luckily my children were not home at the time because I became enraged and screamed, angrily, "Are you freaking kidding me, God? I'm $1,000,000 in debt and this is what you send me? Take this check and stick it where the sun don't shine!"

Bear in mind I was expecting the universe to step in and save me from financial devastation. With that expectation, the check felt like an insult—a cruel joke from the universe. But, almost a year later, remembering that reaction was chilling for me. Knowing what I had learned about the law of attraction, my reaction to the check became the perfect illustration of why I had never manifested more money. After all, if that was my response to a small amount of money, how could the quantum field send me larger amounts?

The quantum field, I knew, had responded as it always does (and always will), "Okay, Greg, I read you loud and clear; you do not want more of this."

I also realized that if I wanted more money, I needed to celebrate what I had, even if it was less than I eventually desired to manifest. Even if only privately, I needed to celebrate any amount of money by raising the roof about it. So I decided that I would make a game out of manifesting pennies on the ground so I could celebrate them like they were going out of style.

Finding a penny was, after all, believable, even in my low emotional state. I decided that I'd manifest pennies and celebrate by telling myself, in the grandest style possible, "Thank you universe, for this special reminder of your infinite abundance and that all good things are possible through you! Thank you for this awesome reminder that you're more than ready to share abundance with me anytime my expectations allow you to! And thank you for this reminder that manifesting anything is as simple for you as manifesting this penny!"

Doing this raised my energy around money every day, even while in the lower emotional perspectives. It kept my spirits raised as I reminded myself that the quantum field would find greater manifestations just as simple once my beliefs were raised. I've got candy jars full of money manifested in this manner because I still play this game today. And I keep the jars in prominent places to remind me of the quantum field's abundance.

You might benefit from a game such as this, even if you don't choose "financial abundance" as a desire you work this process on. If you don't choose pennies, you can easily find something else to play it with. Just make sure you pick an object to manifest that you ordinarily see regularly, encapsulates your desire in some small way, and that you've usually taken for granted or not noticed. Pam, whose story you'll read in the next chapter, desired to find her soul mate. She chose to use couples she saw together out in public as her reminder of the desire she was working to see manifested. And she still privately celebrates this common, everyday occurrence, as a reminder from the universe of the quantum field's infinite abundance.

This game has also taught me that I don't have to take anything for granted—that anything and everything can (and should) be celebrated. Why wouldn't I choose to celebrate anything at all for the miracle it represents and the signpost it exhibits for me of the quantum field's abundance? Where is the rule that states that we are not supposed to find joy in even the smallest of manifestations, despite how much we're accustomed to taking them for granted? As Albert Einstein once said, "There are two ways of looking at the universe: as if nothing is a miracle or as if everything is a miracle."

Another thing I became inspired to do while working my way up the Emotional Reference Chart concerning financial abundance was to ask—and even expect—my lending banks to take less than what I owed to sell the properties. In fact, I also came to ask and expect them to not make me responsible for the mortgage balance remaining after the short sale. I never believed this could be a possible solution during my darker emotional perspective days because, quite simply, I didn't believe myself worthy.

But as I moved up the emotional perspective chart, I began to have a different outlook about myself and saw new possibilities. I started to believe that I was actually doing the bank a favor by arranging for these short sales and debt forgiveness, because I was giving their employees an opportunity to transcend their normally mundane paper-pushing and allow them to help another human being—a human being who was not only grateful, but one who was deserving of such help and wouldn't squander the second chance they were conferring upon him.

Bear in mind, as this process teaches you, your feelings are so much more important than your actions. Not that your actions are unimportant, but how you feel about something will always trump the actions you take to achieve it. Even if you take the greatest action in the world, it cannot overcome your feelings about it.

That said, once my feelings and beliefs were raised, the action for getting short sales was easy and they illustrate the new opportunities I saw, and allowed to manifest, as I moved up the chart. I simply called the lending institution and asked them to do this for me. I knew that every bank that lends money has to deal with default. All these companies have divisions that work with borrowers in, or nearing, default. And, as you just read, I was in a new emotional perspective where I believed myself worthy of such help.

I was always honest with them. Of course I presented the facts in a way that worked in my favor, but I did not lie. The banks had forms for me to fill out. I filled them out promptly and completely, attached a detailed letter explaining my circumstances, and mailed them back the next day.

I gave the banks a week and a half. If I hadn't heard from them, I called them back. If I couldn't speak with the individual reviewing my case, I got the name of that person. Then I began building a relationship with this person—leaving polite, business-like messages and always doing what I said I would do, when I said I was going to do it.

You may say, "Duh, anyone would know to do those things." But I counter by sharing that I was not in a place to do anything like that when I was in the lower emotional states, much less see it as a possibility that might work for me. And, furthermore, how you feel while you perform the actions I've described is the important part. Here are some things I did to make sure I was "feeling worthy" instead of worrying and being afraid, saying, "They'll never do this for me; I don't deserve this and I'm just another deadbeat pest to them."

1. Anytime I contacted the institution, whether via forms I mailed, letters I wrote, or via a telephone call, I made sure I was feeling thusly: "This is going to be a great opportunity for this person to do the things they're really good at and the things they want to do. This person has been waiting for an opportunity to help a deserving person like me—waiting for just this kind of an opportunity to make a difference in a deserving person's life!"

Make sure you're feeling that way any time you find yourself wondering (or worrying) about what the answer to any request you make is going to be. Repeat it over and over until it becomes your expectation anytime you think about the decision maker or the decision-making body.

2. I wrote thank-you letters, in advance, to the person, or people, with whom I was working. As soon as I knew a name, I sat down and pre-wrote that person a detailed thank you letter, thanking them for the exact outcome I desired. I went into detail about how they'd helped a truly deserving individual (me) who will not be wasting the precious second chance they're being given. I addressed this letter and signed it. It was a real letter...that I simply wasn't sending to them yet.

This is an important and powerful process in creating an expectation for a certain outcome that you can use to infuse your process for aligning yourself with any desire. It forces you to walk through all the "they'll never do this for me" fears. Remember: Those fears are only a belief you have—just a simple belief that you can change. You can just as easily believe, "They will do this for me."

I've been amazed at how many of my letters were 100% prophetic. Nostradamus, eat your heart out!

3. Once I had taken the action necessary and I'd performed the techniques I just described here, I forgot about it. I went on and lived my life as if I had no problem—because I didn't. In fact, I took it a step further. I conjured and wrote about exactly how it would feel to achieve my desired outcomes. As I wrote, I reveled in the security, the safety, the elation, and the freedom of those achieved desires. Then, once I'd held those wonderful feelings in my heart, I made a decision to feel that way right now—as often as possible.

I lived my life, to the best of my ability, as if I was already free of my debt—because I was—in my mind, where all physical manifestations originate.

This segues into a common question I get. People ask, "Hey, I was up to writing from the emotional perspective of Joy/Elation and all of a sudden I've been back to feeling depressed. Should I start over again? What's wrong?"

Please understand that the new emotional perspectives you're gaining for the issues about which you're writing are very real. But they're also no more permanent than your old perspectives (you changed those old ones, right?). Each day you have a choice from which perspective you want to live. This process gives you new, more positive choices, but they're still choices.

Don't be discouraged by these "backslides." Remember that old habits die hard...because you've spent a lifetime building neural pathways in your brain. The new ways of thinking are unfamiliar and, often, uncomfortable. Surprising at it is, the familiar pain of old thoughts is often very appealing because of your familiarity with it. That's part of the "human condition."

So don't start from scratch. Manage yourself through the rough patch, reach for the better feeling thoughts (as often as possible from moment to moment), and believe that you're heading in the right direction. A great thing to say to yourself during these times is, "Oh. I'm resisting right now. How curious. I wonder why? I don't need to resist. I wonder where that's coming from?" This self-affirming response puts you right back into acceptance (and you're no longer resisting).

The other morning I was meditating and I had a memory of the movie *The Matrix* in the scene where the protagonist, Neo, enters a room to find a boy bending a spoon with his mind. The boy says, "I don't bend the spoon; I bend everything else."

Leave it to Hollywood to reveal a big secret about the law of attraction. After all, Hollywood is in the virtual reality business. Trying to bend the spoon is one of the major causes of most of the frustrations people have as deliberate creators. Focusing on manifesting the "thing" you want is usually tantamount to trying to "bend the spoon." That's what I was doing when I took all my positive action and started my real estate business.

So how do you "bend everything else"?

Retrain your brain, slowly but surely. Improve your beliefs slowly but surely. Your beliefs, are "everything else." The "thing" you desire (a new car, more money, self-worth, a soul mate, a healthy body, etc.) is the "spoon." That's what I did to finally experience financial abundance (and so many of my other desires since) and that's exactly what you're doing now that you're working this process.

And you'll find that "slowly but surely" means telling yourself ever improving versions of the best-feeling, yet believable, stories you can about everything (and especially those areas or things you desire). Self-worth, as an area around which I raised my beliefs, has been no different than any other. Improved storytelling (as just described) is something I teach extensively in my other books and on my website.

I started around Depression years ago and, with each gradual tick up the Emotional Reference Chart, I manifested new things and saw a new universe, because my energy and perspective was at a new emotional reference point and I was sending new "commands" to the quantum field.

One of the most exciting things about doing this with self-worth, or any other desire, is that it always works, just as quantum physics tell us it will. It works because this is exactly how every single human being creates her physical world every second of every day.

It matters not whether a human being believes this. That is still how she is creating her physical world every second of every day.

So when you become a more powerful intentional creator of your life, as you are learning to do right now, you are not actually "learning" to do something new; you've been doing it all along, every second of your existence. All you're doing is learning to do it more intentionally and more aligned so you can exert greater influence.

Abundance of any kind is not a time-space event, after all. A time-space event is the name physicists give to any material object, because it has left the infinite possibilities of the quantum field and taken a concrete form. Abundance is not a material occurrence. It is not found in our physical manifestations.

Abundance is a state of being. Your physical manifestations reflect your state of being, not vice versa. And every physical manifestation in your life today is merely the result of your previous states of being.

Do not let the cart drive the horse. Do not let your current surroundings dictate your state of being. Your state of being is your decision. Don't try to "bend the spoon." Bend everything around it by retraining your brain and building new beliefs and the "spoon" will bend too. That's the way quantum physics tells us it's supposed to work and that's the way it does work—every time.

And that is why this process is so important. Moving yourself up the emotional chart is you taking control of your state of being in the purest, most impactful manner. This work is you saying, "I will be the one to decide my state of being, thank you. I will not allow my state of being to be dictated by the results of my past perspectives or beliefs. I will create new ones, as I see fit, to align myself with my desires."

If you are like me, you have operated under many illusions your entire life. There are so many illusions that may have hampered, limited, or harmed you—life happening "to" you, scarcity, lack, etc. But perhaps the most damaging illusion is the illusion of failure.

You may fear failure, and no one would blame you if you dread it. Sometimes you choose not to act, simply to avoid the feeling of "failure." Yet failure does not exist; failure cannot exist.

What you have called "failure" is simply an experience of the opposite end of a spectrum—one that is, actually, that very thing or experience you desire. In other words, what you are calling failure is simply another perspective of the thing you desire. Failure is the thing you desire; it's just a different perspective of it.

Here's an example in the form of an experiment. Go to your bathroom sink. Put your hand under your faucet. Turn the hot water handle. The water coming out is cold, right?

Did you begin to grind your teeth, feel constriction and anxiety in your belly, and tell yourself, "See I knew this wouldn't work. I never get what I want!"? Of course not. You know that hot water is on its way. In fact, the very reason you don't get mad is that you know that you are, indeed, feeling hot water that simply hasn't become hot yet.

Does this example sound too simplistic? I propose that you may have been doing the exact opposite of being patient with the "hot water that simply isn't hot yet" regarding many of your desires. You are feeling the "cold water" and focusing on, "This water is cold! This is not working! Where is the hot water?!" It may be subtle and sneaky, but if you are like me, you have been doing that with some of your desires.

Here's a key I discovered from working this process of retraining my brain: You can decide to have no need for the water to turn warm. Choose not to even want the water to turn warm. Instead, simply hold the desire for "warm water" (your desire) and know that it will be so. Know it; don't "need" it. And working this process is a perfect way to practice this perspective.

Isn't that how it has worked for most of your unrealized desires? Haven't you experienced that if you focus on needing or wanting, that's what the universe delivers to you? You "need" and "want" but don't "have"? If you focus on having (and you do have everything—it already exists, in abundance and potential, all around you every second of every day in the eternal and omnipresent quantum field) the universe delivers that to you—and you "have."

This is important. Needing and wanting almost always keep the water cold. Know that the hot water (your desires) is turned on because you're working this process. You are not failing (that is not possible). Through your use of this process of aligning your beliefs with your desires, the hot water is coming. You have just been feeling the opposite side of it for a while.

Keep this in mind while you work this process and you'll start to feel the water warming sooner than you expected.

One last thing about my experience using this process: For my entire adult life I have been goal-oriented. I have always set goals and sought to attain them. Prior to using this process for the first time, I had always been a person who looked for shortcuts to reach my goals. I was the type of person who always felt he could skip or bypass steps that everyone else probably needed to reach a certain goal. I possessed an impatience, borne of self-confidence and desire, which led me to gloss over instructions and proceed toward my goals at a rushed pace in most everything I did.

I've heard this dilemma described as "the smartest guy in the room" syndrome, as if the instructions for achieving a desired outcome are for other people who aren't as smart as me. Because I'm so "special," I can skip right over the directions. Imagine assembling a piece of furniture from IKEA without carefully reading the instructions and you get the idea. I can't tell you how many headaches the trait caused me (and those around me) throughout my life.

Working this process initially was the first time I can remember not looking for shortcuts and, instead, investing myself wholly and completely in the day-to-day instructions without skipping or glossing over anything. I was motivated to do it that way by the loaded gun I had to my head—the impending foreclosures, bankruptcy, and spending the rest of my life in debt. In retrospect, I'm very grateful for that loaded gun because the results of fully investing myself in this process proved to be (as you've read) amazing. And, additionally, I learned that taking no shortcuts is a great way to live; I have practiced this way of doing things ever since with similar results.

If you have ever tried to take shortcuts like I did, I urge you to put aside your desire to attain your desires more quickly. Instead, slow down and fully invest yourself in this process. You may not have a loaded gun to your head, like I did, so your motivation may not be as compelling as mine was. But, regardless of the level of your motivation, I hope you take a cue from me and follow the instructions for this process, as they are written, all the way to the top of the chart.

You'll be very grateful that you did. The quantum field specializes in connecting the dots for you. And it often connects them in very unexpected and unpredictable ways. None of us, in fact, can possibly have the perspective to know exactly how things are supposed to unfold; thinking we have the perspective to label our life events "good" or "bad" is like a wave telling the ocean that it is not breaking correctly. I have no doubt that you'll look back from the top of the emotional perspective chart and see that everything happened just like it was supposed to.

# Chapter Eight—A Coaching Client's Experience with Using My Process for the First Time

I recently coached Pam through this process of retraining her brain, working her way up the Emotional Reference Chart, so her beliefs would be in alignment with her desire for a soul mate. Both of us thought if might be helpful for you to read her experiences with this process. What follows are taken directly from Pam's journal, which she has been so kind to share. For each session, you will find Pam's writing and notes, followed by her notes about my feedback to her.

While your own writing and work might turn out a little different, I hope that reading Pam's journal gives you some additional insight into how this process works in practical, real-time fashion.

## 1st Session

**Pam:** *How am I really feeling in my gut when I think about relationships? That was really easy for me and I had a list of many different things including:*

*Stuck*

*Frustrated*

*Despondent*

*Hopeless*

*Sad*

*Expecting too much/ too high of standards*

*Lonely*

*Insecure*

*Helpless*

*Scared*

*Skeptical*

*Angry*

*Etc.*

**Greg:** *Here are the basics:*

*1. Understanding storytelling. What makes something good or bad is the story you choose to tell yourself about it. Every moment of your life, you are telling a story about every single person, place, event, and circumstance—proclaiming every aspect of your life experience as either good or bad. Words are important. You believe the stories that you tell yourself long enough that they actually become truth for you.*

*2. See your beliefs and feelings objectively and don't pretend you feel better than how you do. It is important to acknowledge feelings and beliefs, just where they are currently, as you also learn at the same time not to personalize them. Beliefs are only your most practiced, habitual thoughts.*

*3. Objectivity without Personifying. If I'm sad I say I'm experiencing sadness in this moment, but sadness is not who I am. I acknowledge the feeling, but I'm not in denial. I am not my feelings. I am experiencing a feeling. Feelings are thermometers for current beliefs.*

*4. How to tell new stories. Calling any story "bad" is just a choice. Anytime you feel bad when experiencing any aspect of your physical reality, or when thinking about dreams and goals, always pay attention. Bad feelings are a signal that your beliefs are not congruent with what you want as the desired outcome.*

*When you encounter a belief that is not aligned with your desired outcome, start where you are and tell a slightly better story.*

## 2nd Session

**Pam:** *Next, on the Emotional Perspective Chart I decided that I was at Doubt/Pessimism in regards to finding a soul mate relationship.*

*I wrote about Doubt.*

*Some examples:*

> *I doubt I can be myself and not conform.*
>
> *I doubt any of the good ones are left.*
>
> *I doubt I can be vulnerable.*
>
> *I doubt this can happen to me. It seems like it is always happening to someone else.*
>
> *I doubt I can have it all: chemistry, healthy living, financially secure, etc.*
>
> *I doubt I can find my "knight in shining armor."*
>
> *I doubt I can find a relationship that fulfills me on all levels.*
>
> *I doubt this process can work. I have tried so many things, so many different times.*
>
> *I doubt he exists.*

*I actually filled two pages with all my doubts. Who would have known there were so many?*

*This isn't where I want to be. I was wondering if I was reinforcing negative things. If a doubtful person looked at this, they would agree.*

*I allowed myself to feel Doubt. I set up camp and really got into Doubt! I allowed myself to be where I was on the chart.*

**Greg:** *Trust you're in the process.*

*Tell yourself, "I believe it could be possible to raise my beliefs but it's okay right now to be at Doubt.*

*Doubt is not where I will be in the long run, but it is okay right now. My mantra.*

*I'm not sugar coating it. I am saying where I am.*

*I am saying a soul mate could be possible. That is where I want to be eventually—and this will be believable to my subconscious and will acknowledge how I feel."*

*Look at the next emotion on the chart and write about your soul mate from that emotion. Pitch a tent in that emotion, just like you did with Doubt.*

*The next one up the chart is Worry (your assignment for the next session).*

*Put yourself into this emotion just like Doubt. Keep writing until you can feel it and know that you're there. Roll around in it. Ignore that this isn't where you want to be, but fully be in Worry.*

*The energy of Worry is higher than Doubt; therefore, you will be at a higher emotional state. It is a tick more positive than Doubt. Once you get into Worry, you will notice, as you go through your day, the universe will manifest different for this one than Doubt. The arrow will be landing a little closer to the bullseye.*

*Stay in Worry and be open to what you find.*

*Think of games that allow the universe to respond to your new emotional state that encourage you.*

*You will experience things regarding relationships that are disappointing but that are a little closer to your goal. It's okay. Spend a day at this perspective and then go up the chart to the next one. It is okay to spend more than one day on each one. Every person is different.*

*Don't move on until you've been at each emotional perspective for at least a day.*

*Which means:*

*Writing about it, reading it, and feeling it and then going out into your day not seeking to jump up the chart. As you go through your day, keep the stories you are telling yourself focused on your emotional reference level.*

## 3rd Session

**Pam:** *Think of games that allow the universe to respond to my new emotional state of Worry:*

*E.g., Look for a smiling person (my reminder from the universe that anything is possible).*

*Greg looked for pennies on the ground.*

*I can decide what someone's smile means. Anything's possible. Stay the course.*

*Seeing a smiling, happy man. Use this as my touchstone—a jolt of hope—a reminder that I am on my way. (Driftwood). It isn't where I will end up, but I am on my way.*

*I put the following on index cards:*

**"Even though I'm disappointed that I don't have a soul mate, I acknowledge that it's possible for me to believe that someday I will experience that. But right now I feel disappointed and it's okay for me to feel disappointed and feel the expectations that arise from this. It's okay to be right where I am. I am in the process and I'm willing to give it a chance and I believe what Greg is sharing with me and I believe it's possible but for right now it's okay for me to be right where I am."**

**"When I interact /converse with a man or see a man on TV (something I feel that I can experience —smiling/ interaction with a man and it feels positive—life, at the office, etc.) I allow that to occur. And when I see them, I will say:**

**'Alright universe, thank you for reminding me and although I'm not where I want to be with manifesting a soul mate, I will stay the course. Thank you for reminding me that you are infinite, abundant, creative, and anything is possible with you and it is easy for me to manifest the perfect partner.' "**

*E.g.,*

*At a grocery store and I see a couple: (self talk)*

*"I bet they are happy, I'm disappointed that I don't have that, but at the same time I acknowledge that it's possible for me to believe that someday I will experience that. But right now I feel disappointed and it's okay for me to feel disappointed and feel the expectations that arise from this. It's okay to be right where I am. I am in the process and I'm willing to give it a chance and I believe what Greg is sharing with me and I believe it's possible, but for right now it's okay for me to be right where I am."*

*That is very believable self-talk. I'm not putting band-aids on anything. I get in there and live it. No need to rush it. Experience the expectations. The universe will be responding.*

*I did this every day. I would look at couples/men, etc., and make up a story and then take out my index cards and finish the story from the emotional perspective where I was. I trusted the process and I knew enough about quantum physics to see what Greg was teaching me. It wasn't easy, but my index cards kept me on track and I could consistently make comments on different situations and scenarios.*

*If I saw a couple in a store that seemed really happy and loving towards each other, when I got back to my vehicle I pulled out my index card and said:*

*"I'm disappointed that I don't have that, but at the same time I acknowledge that it's possible for me to believe that someday I will experience that loving happiness, But right now I feel disappointed and it's okay for me to feel disappointed and feel the expectations that arise from this. It's okay to be where I am. I am in a process."*

*I am very conscious of my interactions with men. After seeing a picture of a man smiling or one of my patients that I am conversing with and having fun with, I would pull out my index card and say:*

*"All right universe, thank you for reminding me and although I'm not where I want to be with manifesting a soul mate, I will stay the course. Thank you for reminding me that you are infinite,*

*abundant, creative, and anything is possible with you and it is easy for me to manifest the perfect partner."*

*Worry:*

Worried because I'm still single after all these years.

Worried that I choose unavailable men.

Worried that I don't have anyone to help me with projects or go to movies or go out to eat with or talk at night with or snuggle with or travel with or cook with, etc.

Worried that my life isn't what I would have imagined it to be.

Worried about my ability to manifest my soul mate. Heaven knows I have put in lots of work trying.

Etc.

*For me, Doubt was easy to write about. Worry was pretty easy, but a little more challenging. Next was Frustration—focusing on what you want and the inability to achieve it at the same time.*

*Maybe I've frustrated myself by trying to do too much.*

*One thing I've noticed since I started the process: There is a path that I am following. I am more focused and deliberate and I am trusting the process. I feel like I have hope—that there is a path. I feel like I'm vibrating at a different level. I'm happier. It's difficult to put into words. I like the commitment that I am continuing to grow and keep moving my perspective higher—a little at a time.*

**Greg:** You might be asking, *"How can the universe manage to overcome all these things that are keeping me from getting from point A to point B?"*

*"How can I believe that? It seems impossible."*

*Frustration is not negative when compared to Doubt.*

*Life is like sitting at a round table and the object of our desire is the centerpiece. Where we are currently sitting is our view of the centerpiece and where I began, my original chair, was Doubt. With each new move up the chart I will move my chair a little to the right and I will see the centerpiece from a slightly different perspective.*

*Frustration—we see for the first time—ambiguity in a tangible way. The definitions, you're finding, do not all have a completely negative connotation.*

*In each emotion there are a variety of perspectives.*

*When Doubt or lower feelings creep up, acknowledge them but say that you are looking at things through the perspective of Frustration. Tell yourself, "Thank you brain. I appreciate your help and I know why I am having these feelings because I have practiced them for so long. But right now I am going to say 'no thanks' to your help."*

*Your brain won't like that because it is a creature of habit. It wants your life to make sense, be predictable (and safe), and make things neat and tidy for you. Unpleasant is okay to the subconscious brain as long as everything remains familiar. But remind yourself gently to go back to Frustration.*

*Some of Frustration doesn't feel that bad. There is tangible and believable hope -the first rays of sunshine poking through.*

*Your subconscious mind will accept Frustration because it is not too positive. You can believe it. We are not trying to jump over the Grand Canyon.*

*My energy is interconnected with everything else.*

*If you wanted to learn to build a house you wouldn't just buy lumber, cement, etc. First you would build the foundation—the structure that holds it up. As you built the foundation, you would learn so much—so that when you tackled the rest of the house you would need to do some more work and learn how to do some new things, but it won't be as difficult because the basic structure would already be there.*

*Tell yourself affirming but believable stories.*

## 4th Session

**Pam:** *I wrote about Frustration*

*E.g.*

> *I am frustrated because I have to try to achieve my results.*
>
> *I am frustrated with all the parts of starting a new relationship: phone calls, emails, etc.*
>
> *I am frustrated with finding a balance in my life for everything.*
>
> *I am frustrated with trying to remember to change my story during the day.*
>
> *I am frustrated with how much time and effort I put towards it.*

*It wasn't a comfortable perspective. It felt strange. I stayed with it and kept changing my story, even though I did not always resonate with it completely.*

*I continue to use my index cards and just change the wording to the Emotional Reference Chart feeling that I am at. I find this tool keeps me on track.*

**"Even though I feel frustrated that I don't have a soul mate, I acknowledge that it's possible for me to believe that someday I will experience that. It's right where I am supposed to be. My only task today is to feel it and embrace it. Feel it, live it, and experience it. I don't have to change it. I don't have to worry about it. I don't have to fix it. I'm not broken, and this is where I am supposed to be. It's okay for me to say that I'm not happy being frustrated, but that's okay too. I can also believe that, just for today, one day at a time, I can keep taking steps forward and I think it is possible that I will get where I want and I'm okay being here with these feeling because they are not who I am."**

*You were right; it definitely feeds more into a positive attitude. There really is not the doom and gloom as there was with Doubt. Now I am at the point of seeing it starting to happen and maybe*

*I'm frustrated because of what I need to do when it does. It definitely puts you into a different energy space.*

*One evening I went to a store and just walked around and observed couples. When I would see a couple and I felt there was something about them that I liked, I would tell myself a better story. And I continued doing that as I wandered around the store looking for different things on my list. Even though I was frustrated because I didn't have that in my life, I acknowledged it. But I also was aware that it was something that I could have in my life.*

*Each time I saw a man that I thought was attractive—my driftwood—I would thank the universe.*

*What we focus on grows, so I really wanted to celebrate those occurrences and that I was open to all this.*

*I then moved on to Discontent. This is going to be a good one, because I can sense this feeling inside of me already.*

*I will continue to tell the stories and interact with men—and acknowledge that the universe is unlimited in what it is providing for me, and that I am exactly where I am supposed to be right at this moment.*

*I wrote about Discontent:*

> *I am discontented because I feel like I've done lots of work on myself but nothing seems to have worked in the area of manifesting my soul mate.*

> *I am discontented because I want to have someone to share my life with.*

> *I am discontented because at times I want to hurry the process along.*

> *I am discontented because I want to live a magical life.*

> *I'm discontented because I feel I have many of the tools to create what I want, yet I just don't use them or I'm not sure how to use them.*

*I am discontented because, in theory, I should have my soul mate.*

**Greg:** *Each perspective is a new tool in our toolbox. Previously we have taken the tools and used them against ourselves. Worry and Frustration, for example, have been in your toolbox and you have used them before and "smacked yourself" with them. You are more comfortable with them, whereas discontent may not have been specifically associated with this desire of wanting a soul mate.*

*There are positive and negative aspects to each perspective. Each perspective has its own energy.*

*You can look back like a mountain climber; you are nowhere near the peak, yet you are where you are supposed to be. You have a destination/goal and you are working your way up like you are supposed to. Each place has a different view—one step at a time. It is nice to look back and see how far you have climbed.*

*The universe is abundant. Even if something isn't exactly what you are looking for, celebrate it anyway—because you are willing to learn and move forward.*

*Not a good idea to meet a mate at this perspective anyway. You want to continue to move up to the higher emotional points and vibrate at those levels.*

*Questions:*

*What other things can you add in besides what you are doing? What inspired actions can you take—like meditation, gratitude journal, creation box, etc.?*

*Definitely mediate a.m. or p.m. When you meditate, you gently and lovingly turn off your brain.*

## 5th Session

**Pam:** *I'm at Indifferent:*

> *I'm indifferent because I feel it should happen faster.*
>
> *I'm indifferent because it's hard for me to stay focused.*

*I'm indifferent because manifesting my soul mate can't be as easy as changing your thoughts and slowly ratcheting up the Emotional Reference Chart.*

*I'm indifferent to the fact that he really exists.*

*I'm indifferent that I can have the life of my dreams.*

*I'm indifferent because I'm wasting my time and maybe I need to be proactive.*

*These feel very believable to me. I have captured a glimpse of what it is that I want somehow—I have tasted it in some way. So I am doubting that it can emerge in the grand form that I want it to be.*

*This is real, but I haven't seen it as applied to a soul mate. I have had many manifestations in other areas. I just have not seen my soul mate come into my life.*

*Index card:*

**"Although I feel indifferent about it, it's okay to be right where I am. I know that there is some inherent positivity in Indifference, and I also know that Indifference is a more positive perspective than where I have been with my soul mate, and I also acknowledge that it is okay to be here and to feel both the wanted and unwanted thoughts that come along with Indifference. The unwanted feelings are okay. I don't need to deny them or beat myself up for having them or pretend that I don't have them. It is okay, brain, to have those thoughts—because those thoughts are the natural expectations that come from any belief."**

**Greg:** *This is where you are, but you won't stay there. Life is becoming more magical because life is at a higher perspective. The positive energy will continue to grow and get better. The beliefs are changing slowly.*

*It's never not okay to be right where you are. So you won't sabotage anything by being there.*

*Carry around a notepad and journal about your perspective. Revel in it. Don't beat yourself up for being where you are. Don't deny that you are there. Don't say you shouldn't ever have a negative thought.*

*When you change/raise your beliefs, your expectations also change. It is a slow and believable process; therefore, your subconscious brain will believe the new beliefs and adopt them. Positive thought you did in the past? Your subconscious brain allowed those things to make you feel good but didn't accept them as your true beliefs. Now your subconscious brain is saying, "Yes I can believe Indifference." You are tricking your subconscious brain.*

*Your subconscious brain is concerned with basic desires.*

*When you meet the man you marry, there will be lots of reasons why you will marry that man (logical justifications) but the real, and only, reason will be because you love him. And that real reason will come from your subconscious brain.*

*You are leading your subconscious brain along, like leaving a trail of carrots for a bunny. A scared bunny will not jump into your house because you coaxed him in. You have to stand still, add carrots slowly, and continue to move back and lay carrots, etc. The bunny will come into your house one step at a time. If you tried to go for the gusto with positive expectation, it wouldn't come. That would be too fast. So with Indifference you are taking one step closer.*

*Remind yourself during the day that it is not a negative thing. You are not in a place where you are not supposed to be.*

## 6th Session

**Pam:** *I got a little side tracked wondering why so many people have a partner and I don't. I realized that I have to tell a different story, but it is challenging at times. Ideas?*

**Greg:** *Our feelings aren't facts unless we make them facts. They aren't to be ignored or stuffed or hidden away. They are a feedback loop for our beliefs. When you are not feeling very* *happy/joyful, it is almost always true that you are doing better than you are feeling.*

*Your feeling is only what you are experiencing in this moment. It is not who you are. It is not your state of being—unless you allow it to be.*

*These experiences can be very helpful. First, take away the power of what you are feeling right now. It is easy for feelings to hold a lot of power over us. Right now, instead of saying, "I feel unworthy," you are saying, "I am unworthy." You have the pain of being the feeling rather than experiencing the feeling. One is painful. The other is suffering.*

*Suffering is always optional. If we are personifying the emotion, we are suffering.*

*1. Write about how you are feeling right now. Dump it on the page. Go for it. Don't hold anything back. After that is all down on the page, sit back and say, "This is how I feel in this moment. These feelings are not who I am. They are not to be ignored or denied but they are not who I am."*

*2. How are they related to feeling indifferent about having a soul mate? Frame it within this perspective. Why is it that all this happened this weekend? Is it related to where I am in regards to my emotional perspective?*

*3. Write your soul mate a funny, grateful letter.*

*4. Find gratitude for what you have.*

*You manifested a different reality because of your perspective and reacted to it from that perspective, which would have been different at a lower perspective. You may look back at it as a pivotal weekend.*

*Coincidences are the universe's way of keeping its anonymity.*

*If you can't find a blessing, withhold judgment.*

## 7ᵗʰ Session

**Pam:** *Yesterday I had an incident with my vehicle. I was quite devastated and again was wondering what the heck was going on. The person responsible was very kind and apologetic and was willing to do anything to make everything work out perfectly. So, I started telling myself a better story and it included that person. It was about how kind some people are and even though this is a major hiccup in my life is not a tragedy and things will get taken care of quickly. And that is exactly what happened. I was leaving on a trip in two days and really wanted to take my own vehicle. They were pretty sure it would not be available before I left. But, I kept visualizing it being here, telling a different story and keeping focused on what I wanted. I had decided to get a rental car the day before I was to leave (I guess I did not have unwavering faith:0) and there were constant road blocks coming up when I tried to secure the rental car. I was on the phone with the rental car agency when I was handed a note that said "YOUR VEHICHLE IS READY"... A day ahead of schedule.*

*My Story:*

*"Although I really would have preferred to not have this experience, I can believe it's possible that I lack the perspective to see that everything happened exactly the way it was supposed to and I can be willing, just for today to withhold final judgment and just trust that it might be so."*

*I'm moving up the chart to Pensiveness. Very challenging to write about it.*

*I looked at pensiveness as restlessness.*

> *I am pensive because it doesn't seem to be moving fast enough—a snail's pace is how I feel it is moving.*

> *I am pensive because I'm doing the same thing over and over.*

> *I am pensive because waiting isn't my style.*

> *I am pensive because staying focused and on track is challenging.*

*I am pensive because sometimes I'm forgetting to do the "program."*

**<u>Greg:</u>** *It was an interaction with a man and he was very nice, kind, etc.*

*We need to stay as neutral as possible and stay the course.*

*Look for the positives and things will flow.*

*Story about peanut butter sandwich smeared on sidewalk:*

*Today I was walking down the sidewalk in Old Louisville. On the sidewalk, there was one small spot of peanut butter. Yet the small spot was only about 2 feet away from the rest of the peanut butter sandwich. There were about 100 ants all around that one little spot of peanut butter, frantically trying to get as much as they could. But if they only knew that about 2 feet away there was this huge amount of peanut butter, and it probably could feed the colony for a relatively long time, they wouldn't have been so frantic. This story is very similar to us, we are just focused on one thing and not realizing that a little ways away there's a solution that is so close.*

*There were some good lessons to all that were involved.*

*Pensive—neutral—won't spark a lot of passion—passive.*

## 8<sup>th</sup> Session

**<u>Pam:</u>** *When you are pensive, you are restless. There are many reasons I was restless about not having a soul mate yet. It catapulted me back into doing the process again. When I saw people together, I would tell a different story from the perspective of Pensive and I would thank the universe for the driftwood that I was getting each day.*

*Next emotional reference point—I feel like I am crossing the bridge. I feel like Pensive is the bridge and now I am going over the bridge and it is getting more positive.*

*Acceptance:*

*I'm accepting because I know I'm doing the process to move me closer to finding my soul mate.*

*I'm accepting because I'm on the more positive side of the Emotional Reference Chart.*

*I'm accepting because I'm more at peace with the process.*

*I'm accepting because deep down inside I feel like I'm making progress towards attracting my soul mate.*

**Greg:** *The perspective of Pensive is neutral—not positive or negative. When you meet someone, it is whom you are manifesting from your perspective. When you meet someone, you can just go with it because he is someone to learn from even though he is not "the one"—because you're meeting him at the lower-than-optimal emotional perspective you are at now.*

*Everything you see and experience is a reflection of what's inside you. Every day, when you get up, say, "I am going to walk out into this world and see what my reflection looks like—won't that be interesting?" Smile and see what happens. It will be inspiring to you in small but noticeable ways. Continue to journal emotional points.*

*Acceptance can be intimidating because it is easier to write from a negative emotional reference point and now you are going more into positive. All you have to do now, in this process, is what you have been doing all along. A higher emotional reference point is scarier because you have not been there. Acceptance is not all positive (it represents the status quo), and you're not quite to your desires.*

*For example, while writing a book, there are many stages. When I get close to finishing it, sometimes I put it down for a while, because there is some comfort in letting it sit unfinished. The book is still in the comfort zone of "someday," and I'm not yet putting it out there to succeed or fail. And then when I push it into the next stage I am out of my comfort zone.*

*It's easy to get trapped in the same comfort zone when we reach these new, higher emotional perspectives.*

## 9th Session

**Pam:** *Moved into Hopeful during vacation.*

*Hopeful*

> *I'm hopeful that I'm getting closer to the higher vibration of the chart.*

> *I'm hopeful because I've been diligently applying what Greg is teaching me.*

> *I'm hopeful because my heart is opening up.*

> *I'm hopeful because I'm becoming more at peace with myself and what will be.*

> *I'm hopeful because somehow I know that this process is working just like it's supposed to.*

*Note card information:*

*"I currently feel hopeful but I believe, with practice and effort, I can learn to tell better stories about hopeful over time. I consciously choose to tell better stories about hopeful. I believe that, with time, my beliefs will change about it and so will my material reality and experiences concerning it. I believe that the universe is creative, unlimited, and all things are possible."*

*When traveling, men would come over and ask if I needed anything and they were very attentive and nice. Everywhere I went people were extremely nice - One man told me a story about his daughter who gave him sunscreen with glitter in it....very funny. I was more aware of how much people, men in general, were conversing with me.*

**Greg:** *You have the feeling that something great is going to happen. You are not inundated with negative feelings. You are feeling hopeful.*

*Everything in the physical world comes from the quantum field and is put together with different combinations of hydrogen, oxygen, carbon, and nitrogen atoms. It is all an exchange of energy. We have influence over our reality. What we often fail to realize is that the quantum field responds to what we are, not necessarily what we want.*

*For example, when we ride a bus, we don't say we own the bus, and ride it everywhere, because that would be silly. We already own a vehicle. We're just riding the bus temporarily, because we've chosen to. The former, however, is what most of us do with our lives. We look around at our current manifestations and we define our state of being by them. I have an empty bank account; that means I'm poor. I'm alone; therefore, I'm not worthy of a mate. I have a job that I hate; therefore, I'm not capable of having a dream job, etc.*

*The manifestations we have at this moment are the reflections of previous emotional reference points.*

*Our beliefs are rocks we throw into the water, and the rings made by the splash are the manifestations.*

*Nothing is in the same place for more than a few seconds.*

*You can give yourself positive affirmations all day long, but until your beliefs change you will not be manifesting a soul mate like you truly desire.*

## 10th Session

**Pam:** *Moving up to Anticipation/Eagerness:*

> *I'm eager because I'm becoming clearer with what I want to attract in a soul mate. I have made my list and checked it twice.*

> *I'm eager because I'm becoming more familiar with the process of deliberate creation.*

> *I'm eager because I've been seeing more "driftwood" in my life.*

*What somebody does isn't as important as who they are!*

*I walked into the grocery store today and I was behind an older couple and they were holding hands and I just wanted to take out my cell phone and take a picture of them because it was so amazingly cool and inspirational. So I told myself a story about this as I walked behind them.*

**Greg:** *When you get up to Eagerness you can begin to ask questions:*

*"I wonder what amazing experiences I will have today."*

*Before I married, I never asked dates what they did for a living. I'm not interested in what you do; I'm interested in who you are.*

*It's natural to be optimistic about meeting someone.*

*When you park your car at a store, pose a question:*

*"I wonder what really cool experience I will have when I go into the store?"*

*Celebrate what we want when we see it. If there is a woman in a relationship that you want to emulate, or if there is a man you want to get to know better, celebrate simply seeing them.*

*Ask yourself, "I wonder how awesome it will be to meet a man who is...."*

*Think of a sculptor and how she starts. She starts with a big lump of clay and then sculpts it into something beautiful. It is the same with relationships. When you start you don't know where you're going. And then you meet different people and you refine and determine more what you want because of the experiences you have.*

## 11th Session

**Pam:** *I am continuing with Eagerness. I set an intention for talking with someone when I went into the grocery store. I bought some coconut water and could not carry it all out at one time. A guy was standing there and offered to carry it out to my vehicle for me. He was a farmer and he was telling me about how he put his calves' medicine in coconut water. It was a fascinating and fun conversation. I really enjoyed it a lot.*

*A fun thing happened. A gentleman (85 years old) was very complimentary telling me how lovely/beautiful I was, etc. I smiled because it was so nice to hear those things, but the story I told myself was about getting the same compliments from a man closer to my desired age.*

**Greg:** *Continue to question things from this positive reference point. Remember to ask the question because the universe will answer it for you. Stay with eagerness as long as you need to.*

*When you move up the chart, you send the universe different energy. You will meet people who are more closely aligned to being your soul mate. The longer you practice it, the more you experience things being more like, or aligned with, what you desire.*

*Use any tools at your disposal to increase your energy and make you feel very good. You will be amping up your vibration. Write a thank-you letter in advance for the things that you want to happen. Write a note or letter to your partner, looking back and expressing your gratitude for him in your life. Create a void in a positive way. Like water, it will fill.*

## 12th Session

**Pam:** *Moved up to Confidence. I found I was struggling about moving up the chart because I was afraid of failing or not manifesting my soul mate. It feels like it is getting more serious now. I think I was beginning to put more expectations on myself.*

*I'm doing meditation once a day more consistently.*

*I wrote down the things I appreciated in my life and then took about 10-15 minutes and focused on those and felt really good about having those things in my life. It's similar to meditation, but instead of quieting my mind, I was focusing my mind on appreciation and gratitude.*

**Greg:** *One way of illustrating this is saying that now you know how to paint a portrait. Two years from now you will be that much better and you will look back and say that, yes, you knew how to* *paint a portrait then, but look at how much better you are now. You are stepping into new territory. You're very used to the emotions of doubt and frustration, and that was more familiar to you, but when you get into the higher emotional perspectives this is very unfamiliar territory and it can be a little scary at times.*

*You will continue to get better and better at it. Just like painting, you will get better and better, but there will still always be room for improvement.*

*Celebrate each small thing. Create opportunities to celebrate relationships.*

*Seeing happy people, in relationships or otherwise, in stores, billboards, commercials, etc.*

*Celebrate to get more of it! What you celebrate will grow.*

*Invent a game—turn on the TV—see a loving couple—celebrate! It is your perception, belief, expectation.*

*The physical reality that we see today are the ripples in the water that were created by the expectations that we threw into the pond a day, a week, or a year ago.*

*When we try to figure out, "How in the world can that ripple (I want) find its way to me?"—we are getting in the way of the universe's job.*

*Consider this scenario. You decide to go for a walk to clear your head. Instead of going your normal route, you choose a slightly different route. You're walking by a house you've never seen before and a guy is wheeling his garbage out to the curb. He is handsome and your eyes meet and he starts up a conversation with you. He is visiting his sister who lives in that house. Wow. That's how the universe usually works. It's unpredictable and amazing.*

## 13th Session

**Pam:** *I am at LOVE right now and things are going extremely well. I have had lots of insights and things have been happening that are so cool.*

*My birthday was an absolutely wonderful, amazing, spectacular, giggly, fun day. I celebrated the day with friends and family. We laughed and laughed and laughed. I can't remember giggling and laughing so much. It just did a body good to have so much fun. It was a great day.*

*I have had some realizations during my quiet times:*

*I'm continuing to refine my vibration and send the Universe a clearer image on what I want. I know I need to trust the Universe. I realize that "finding love" has to do with your vibration and you really shouldn't try to find it, you should let it find you. I will focus on living my life with passion, telling better stories and having as much fun as I can and refining what it is that I really want in a partner by paying attention to what I like about the current men in my life. I really want to get to the point where I'm having so much fun that I don't even notice that I am single anymore. I know that when I am at that point I will be vibrating "I'm happy, whole and complete" and the Universe won't be able to help but bring me more situations that help me feel that way and THAT'S when the guy will show up - my vibrational match. Just thinking out loud here!*

*I am really liking LOVE - it seems like things have opened up and really started to shine out.*

**Greg:** *"Don't handcuff the universe" by placing requirements on the fulfillment of your desires—by requiring its manifestation in a specific manner or in a specific time-frame.*

*Love is merely the beginning of the journey, not the end.*

*Don't put any pressure on yourself.*

*The universe responds to your beliefs.*

*Even if you are at Love, there are still rocks in the stream. You will lift up the one rock, someday, that is holding back your soul mate. So continue to tell yourself the best-feeling, believable story, like:*

*"Yes, I definitely want a soul mate and to be honest I wish I had a soul mate right now. Sometimes I feel a little disappointed,*

*sometimes I feel a little sad, and sometimes I feel a little angry that he is not standing here, I want to be honest about that. I also know that my life is darn good and my experiences are aligned with my desires and I have nothing to complain about in that regard. And I know that I fully understand and embrace that it's my beliefs that allow my life experiences to be even more aligned. I won't have to decide who and when because it is not about that—I can let it go and relax and I can be open to whatever opportunities I encounter today to grow me. I know, I have faith, and I trust that as I continue to play this game and be open to those opportunities that these things will happen to me just as surely as other things have."*

*Soul mate is such a strong desire—don't dampen this desire by pretending you're okay with not having one. Not even for self-protection.*

*Keep playing the game and it will come when you let go of whatever it is that you are holding onto.*

*Now, for the rest of your life, you get to play the awesome game: "Grow a Greater Pam." Acknowledge how you feel—don't act like you don't want it to happen now. Tell the story as it is.*

*"Although I really hope that it is not going to take me three years to manifest my soul mate, and this is really how I feel, I also can accept today that, however long it takes, I'm going to be okay, I'm going to have everything I need and I'm going to have a dang good time with my life. I'm going to be happy."*

*You are in the process now and life is good.*

Now seems like a good time to share a story I told Pam recently. It has to do with working yourself up the top of the Emotional Reference Chart and still not manifesting exactly what you desire.

When I wrote my story about using this process on financial abundance, I saved this part until the end of the book, because it pertains to being at the highest emotions. During my first time working this process, I had been at Love/Ecstasy for about five months and, during those five months, I was able to let go of 14 of my rental properties, never declared bankruptcy, and had almost no remaining debt. I write "almost no remaining debt" because I still had one property that I just could not seem to sell (even though I had been told by my bank that they would consider a short sale on it though there were no promises to forgive me of the debt remaining after any such short sale).

During those five months, I just couldn't figure out why that one property remained, hanging over my head as a possible foreclosure and relatively massive assigned debt (the mortgage was about $90,000). I truly was living the emotional reference point of love. The proof of that was not only found in the miraculous resolutions of all my other properties, but also in the other successes I was having in my life. Although I couldn't figure out what the problem was, I was confident the final resolution for it lay close enough that it would happen for me eventually.

I had massive faith in not only how our universe manifests our physical reality, but also in the process I had been using. I knew the universe had to eventually respond to my emotional perspectives, or beliefs, of "love" regarding money, I just had no idea when or how it would. To that end, I stayed open to discovering the problem that was still blocking the resolution of this final rental property and knew I would address it directly when it became clear.

During those five months, I continued to keep my emotional reference point high regarding money and I also continued to play games to help me stay there. I continued to tell myself the best-feeling believable stories about the property like: "Although I am not happy that I still have this one remaining property and although I am frustrated that I haven't been able to release it from my physical reality, I know the universe will eventually respond to my new beliefs about money. I know everything is happening just like it's supposed to, even when it's not happening the exact way I want it to. And I know that I'm committed to doing whatever it takes to release this last property, so I will continue to stay open to whatever I find or however I'm motivated to do it."

In May, 2008, I got a call from my realtor on a Thursday afternoon. He told me that a potential buyer had offered $10,000 for the property and expressed his ardent pessimism that the bank would accept such a low offer. But he said he would be submitting the offer anyway because we had nothing to lose. The worst the bank could do, after all, was say "no."

It just so happens that a friend invited me to a spiritual retreat that very weekend. When I went to the retreat, the men built a bonfire on Friday night—where the weekend's activities were explained. I learned that on Saturday morning, there was a workshop entitled, "Who Do You Need to Forgive?". I knew exactly who I needed to forgive, but I didn't want to so I decided not to attend.

You see, early in the summer of 2007, my wife and I divorced. Of course, in any divorce, no one party is completely responsible for the dissolution of the marriage, and mine was no exception. I did, however, still harbor quite a bit of resentment and anger toward my ex-wife. And my honest assessment was that I wasn't ready to let go of that anger.

Sitting around that bonfire, my friend said to me, "Who do you need to forgive?" I told him I needed to forgive my ex-wife and that I wouldn't be going to the workshop because I wasn't yet willing to do that. My friend shared that he had similar feelings about needing to forgive his father. He asked me to make a pact with him and attend the workshop together. As his friend, I agreed but not without some trepidation.

It turns out I was very glad I attended that workshop. During it, I was reminded that the real reason to forgive someone is for ourselves. Carrying around anger and resentment toward someone is like me drinking a deadly (spiritual) poison and hoping they die. If we love ourselves, if we have enough self-worth to be free, I was reminded, we owe it to ourselves to let go. Not because we condone what that person did, but because we're no longer willing to commit the emotional suicide of holding on to our anger.

I left the workshop ready to let go of my resentment. That night, the men built a huge bonfire. Each workshop participant was invited to share about something they needed to let go of and, symbolically, throw a totem into the fire—signifying the act of letting it go. When my turn came, I shared all about my ex-wife and my anger toward her. I shared about how my anger had been defining me and, also, weighing heavily on me. Through many tears, I threw my totem into the fire when I finished sharing.

As I left the workshop with my friend on Sunday, I felt like a tremendous spiritual weight had been lifted off me. I felt completely free for the first time in a long time. It was a beautiful experience, and I was very grateful I had the opportunity to do it.

Driving my son to soccer practice the very next day, I got a phone call from my realtor. When I saw his name on the caller ID, I knew what he was going to tell me even before I answered. And I was correct. With astonishment in his voice, my realtor told me, "Greg, you're not going to believe this, but the bank accepted the $10,000 offer! And they're also not going to assign the balance of the mortgage debt to you. You're done. All your properties have been sold and you're free!"

I thanked my realtor and whooped it up with excitement enough to startle my son. But although I was happy and excited, I also wasn't surprised. I knew that I would be removing the obstacle keeping my last property around my neck, I just didn't know when or how I would do it. It was, therefore, no surprise to me at all when I learned that letting go of my anger toward my ex-wife was, indeed, that final obstacle. And I had firmly removed it that weekend.

(By the way, after my financial dilemmas were cleared away, I worked this process on self-worth with amazing results)

You see, even when we are at the highest points on the Emotional Reference Chart, there can still be beliefs, issues, or feelings that will block the unimpeded flow of our desires from manifesting from the quantum field. For me, my anger had been like a big rock in that stream of good will—not large enough to prevent most of my desires from manifesting but sizeable enough to impede the full flow and manifestation of them. Letting go of my anger was tantamount to taking a big rock out of a fast-moving stream and giving the water a clear, unobstructed path to flow.

You, too, may not see the immediate, complete manifestation of your desires just because you have worked your way up to Love on the Emotional Reference Chart. In my case, I still would have been happy with getting rid of 14 of my 15 rental properties— but I'm very grateful I rid myself of my "big stone" and manifested my desires exactly as I hoped. If you get to Love and find some parts of your dream or desire inhibited from your material reality, you, too, probably have some lurking resistance that's hidden from your conscious awareness.

This is exactly why I say that using this process will make you much more aligned with your desires, not completely aligned. It may be that, to be completely aligned, you need to continue raising your beliefs from the perspective of Love and release some lingering resistance. This is also why I call this process an exciting game (called "Grow a Greater You") that you get to play for the rest of your life. When you reach Love on the Emotional Reference Chart, your playing of this amazing game hasn't ended. In fact, it's just begun.

So you should not become overly frustrated or throw in the towel if your desires are not manifested, completely and totally, just because you are at the top of the emotional chart. Just begin to play the game "Grow a Greater You" from the amazing perspective of Love. With willingness and an open mind, you will eventually be inspired to take the action(s) necessary to release any resistance and expand fully into the total manifestation of your desires.

Pam, you might like to know, has met an amazing man. He is handsome, kind, smart, successful, a lot of fun, and shares many of Pam's most important interests. He derives as much pleasure and happiness being around Pam as she does being with him, yet he has a life of his own and, to her delight, doesn't depend on Pam to make him happy. In fact, this man is almost a perfect match to the letters Pam pre-wrote to him back during the time she was first writing about her soul mate from the initial positive emotions on the emotional perspective chart.

Pam is thrilled, yet not really surprised. Her current romance is not something she feels unworthy of. In fact, today Pam knows that this man is nothing more (nor less) than a perfect reflection of who she has become—a person with ever deepening beliefs of love and appreciation about herself and about having a soul mate. Pam has truly become the living embodiment of the soul mate she once felt she needed. So manifesting this man is a natural result of how the quantum field works. Although it is magic and at one time seemed nearly impossible for her, it is no more unbelievable than anything else Pam experiences in her successful life.

Pam has met many wonderful men since getting to the top of the chart. In fact, she expects to continue attracting cool, fun men into her life. And her perspective has changed so that she no longer needs one lifetime soul mate to make her happy. She is providing herself with the happiness she sought from a soul mate and, thus, wonders if her soul mate might not wind up being several men instead of her preconceived notion of only one man. Perhaps there is no such thing as "the one," Pam imagines. In fact, Pam continues to meet men she would have "settled" for back when she "needed" a soul mate—but her desires have continued to grow and she has enough self-worth now that she is completely comfortable with being her own source of happiness.

Pam, like me, is on the journey of playing "Grow a Greater You" from the top of the chart. It's a life-long journey and it is also a fun one—full of amazing insights, perspectives, and inspirations.

Pam reports that getting to a place where she no longer "needed" her soul mate to be happy was the "big rock" which she needed to remove from her stream of good will and abundance. In other words, after reaching the emotional perspective of Love through this process of retraining her subconscious brain to have new beliefs aligned with her desires for a soul mate, Pam continued to grow and expand. She continued to play the game, "Grow a Greater Pam." Her current flame did not appear immediately but, instead, came into her life as she was able to remove the obstacle of "needing" him.

Pam is happier today than she can ever remember. And her wonderful man is not the source of that happiness; she is the source of her happiness. At the end of the day, this became the final, big secret Pam uncovered about having a soul mate—during her own journey up the emotional perspective chart and beyond. This was the "big rock" Pam was finally able to remove from her stream because of all the work she'd done with this process. Her man, whom she once envisioned as the primary source of all the wonderful feelings Pam desired (and is now experiencing), ended up being merely another important part of the joyful life Pam now lives.

By continuing to play "Grow a Greater Pam" from the highest emotional perspectives on the chart, Pam has manifested one of her greatest and longest absent desires. And she did so in ways she never could have imagined from her previous, lower emotional perspectives (or beliefs). To hear her tell it, she originally imagined that her soul mate would appear as a separate and distinct entity from her and give her feelings of love, happiness, safety, security, joy, peace, completeness, and serenity.

But now, having manifested this man, Pam tells a different story. Her soul mate is nothing more nor less than a logical extension of who she has become and her beliefs—reflecting back her own feelings of love, happiness, safety, security, joy, peace, complete-ness, and serenity that she has for herself. This man is not, it turns out, a separate and distinct entity from her who has manifested to give her what she desires; this man is a simple and perfect reflection of who Pam is.

I'm excited that you are now joining Pam, me, and hundreds of others on this amazing journey to the realization of your greatest desires. I am thrilled that you, too, are removing the barriers and obstacles that kept you suffering for so long—so that you, too, can align your beliefs with your desires and fulfill some of your most fervent, and painfully absent, desires. I can't predict exactly how and when your desires will come to fruition, just as I couldn't have for Pam or even myself. But I know that if you stay the course with this process, it will happen for you if invest yourself into this process completely and continue to play the life-changing game "Grow a Greater You."

The quantum field specializes in manifesting our expectations into our physical reality. That is what it does, without fail, as surely as the sun will rise tomorrow. It knows how to connect the dots for us perfectly and amaze us with unexpected and unpredictable manifestations that will amaze and astound you, now that you've learned how to allow it to by retraining your subconscious brain. Welcome to the first day of the rest of your life—a life that will be forever altered and different in the most spectacular ways. Welcome to your own personal game of "Grow a Greater You."

Game on!

# Chapter Nine - About the Author

Greg Kuhn is a professional educator and an author. He has worked for duPont Manual High School since 2000 and has written seven books about human development and success. Greg lives in Louisville, Kentucky, and is the author of the best-selling "Why Quantum Physicists..." book series.

Greg's wonderful wife is an artist and a high school art teacher. He has four amazing sons, one by marriage. He couldn't write books without a wife willing to inspire him and without his sons' cooperation.

## Greg's other titles are:

Why Quantum Physicists Don't Get Fat

Why Quantum Physicists Do Not Fail

Why Quantum Physicists Create More Abundance

Why Quantum Physicists Do Not Suffer

Why Quantum Physicists Play "Grow a Greater You"

The 30-Minute Soulmate

Each book is available on Amazon.

Greg does speaking engagements as his schedule allows. Contact him through:

Twitter: @KuhnGregory
Instagram: @gregoryskuhn1967
Facebook: https://www.facebook.com/whyquantumphysicists/
Website: www.whyquantumphysicists.com

Made in the USA
Monee, IL
16 July 2020